Illustrations by Nishan Akgulian

weldon**owen**

How to run around less & enjoy life more

WORKING MOM

[SURVIVAL GUIDE]

Suzanne Riss & Teresa Palagano

FOREWORD BY DR. MICHELE BORBA

WORKING MOTHER magazine

foreword *page* **4**   introduction *page* **7**   our survey *page* **10**

1 Here Comes Baby *page* **12**

page **28**

5 Look Inside *page* **60**

Mom on the Run **6** *page* **76**

8 Tech Time *page* **104**

9 Navigating Now *page* **116**

Back to Work **2**

page **38** On-the-Job Survival **3**

page **50** Strategic Alliances **4**

As They Grow page **92** **7**

Work Anywhere **10** page **130**

index *page* **140**   acknowledgments *page* **143**

Less work for working moms

Though my three sons are grown now, I was a working mom throughout their young lives—a teacher, educational psychologist, parenting and child expert, consultant, and writer. I've always found great joy in having a career, but I sure wish I'd had this guide then to help with the balancing act. I would have multitasked less, been "in the moment" more, and made "me time" a priority. I would have felt more pride and less guilt over my decision to be a working mom. I would have found it easier to admit that I really loved my work—I still do. I see myself in these pages, and I know that the challenges and frustrations, the rewards and joys that are explored here will be instantly familiar to any working mom.

As parents, we want to do everything we can to help our children be happy. We hope to nurture them and equip them with the skills they'll need to lead fulfilling lives and to be good citizens of the world. But these days, many parents, working moms in particular, face more pressures than ever before. We sometimes feel at a loss about what to make a priority, what to let slide, and how to handle the pulls we feel from so many directions as we try to do our best for our families and our careers.

And while we all strive to be great moms, great employees, great partners, and great friends, we can't be great at everything every single day. What helps is making reasonable choices, finding shortcuts that actually make things easier, accepting less-than-immaculate homes, and taking advantage of strategies from moms who have been there.

The *Working Mom Survival Guide*, written by Suzanne Riss and Teresa Palagano, is a wonderful resource for working moms,

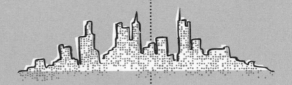

offering a repository of tips and tools. Uplifting and inspiring, this book will help you find perspective and humor in the face of challenges that might otherwise make you feel like crawling under the covers. The information is accessible—you can flip through a chapter and pull out the golden nuggets you're seeking fast. You'll discover helpful strategies on everything from navigating your career while raising kids to building strong, supportive networks so that you have a safety net when inevitable crises strike. Time-saving tips you haven't heard about before are peppered throughout the book, making it possible to find more time to spend with your family.

I've contributed to *Working Mother* magazine for many years, serving as an expert source for stories on everything from raising ethical children to bully-proofing your grade-schooler. What I don't think the editors realize is that I learn from them too, both from the magazine and now from this book.

Suzanne and Teresa convey a pride in working, in contributing financially to one's family, and in serving as role models to children that is sure to resonate. They show how being a mom can up your game at work. (After all, do you know a mom who doesn't excel at multitasking, planning, and being organized?) They celebrate the fact that working benefits your health and boosts your self-esteem. They embrace the ambitious mom who attends her daughter's soccer practice and also goes for the big promotion. They remind us that a better title can increase your ability to advocate for other working parents. Be prepared: Your self-esteem may soar as you read these pages.

I also appreciated the *Working Mom Survival Guide*'s chapter on new media, which offers insights I'm all in favor of but haven't read anywhere else. We so often think of ways to limit our kids' screen time, but we don't always realize how our own screen time affects them. Our kids notice when we're always on our BlackBerry or constantly texting the office. Here, you'll find insightful, realistic tips on how to unplug so you can enjoy more face-to-face time with your children. It's a gentle approach that provides simple solutions that help moms find a balance between home and work.

Suzanne and Teresa know that working moms too often place their own needs on the very bottom of their to-do lists. They recognize how important it is for busy moms to nurture themselves. By the time you've finished the last chapter, you'll feel less anxious and guilty, and you'll see that self-care is actually quite selfless. Happy moms who take care of themselves and feel fulfilled bring more joy into their homes.

These days, working is an essential part of finding happiness for many women. Working moms enjoy feeling useful and contributing to their family's financial well-being. And of course, if you want to teach your children how to be independent and follow their passions, you serve as a powerful role model when you do the same.

Michele Borba, EdD
Parenting expert, educational psychologist,
Today show contributor, and award-winning
author of *The Big Book of Parenting Solutions*

Sharing — mom to mom

During a recent Sunday-evening phone call to finalize a book chapter, our conversation kept getting interrupted: "Jay, drop that ax right now. Hold on, my kid's trying to kill his playdate with a Nerf sword." "Jack, honey, where did you last see Woody's hat?" Once the pull-string cowboy had his red hat back on straight and the swashbucklers were sent their separate ways, we got back to work. Until one of us had to run because "Damn, the raviolis are exploding."

Both of us worked at *Working Mother* from when our sons, Jack and Jay, were toddlers through age 7. And as we planned each issue, we had the good fortune to be able to plumb our own concerns, quandaries, and frustrations for stories—and seek practical solutions that have, on many occasions, rescued us. What's a working mom to do when her child asks, "Why can't you be the class mom? Why do I have to go to daycare every day after school? Why won't your cell phone stop buzzing?"

Talks about our kids and careers have led to lots of survival dos and don'ts. As we learned strategies from the experts we consulted regularly, the thousands of in-the-trenches moms we tapped from our reader panel, and all the studies that crossed our desks, we realized we'd become a repository of valuable work-life tips: Everything from how to negotiate flextime (hint: trial period) to how to de-wrinkle a shirt without an iron (hint: spray-on fabric softener). The *Working Mom Survival Guide* grew out of our desire to spread the wealth, to share the information that was so generously shared with us.

There was another reason too—as working moms, we know that we benefit from all the support we can get. The United States hit a tipping point in 2011 when, for the first time, women officially outnumbered men in the workforce. Mothers are now the primary or co-breadwinners in almost two-thirds of American families. There are almost 10 million single moms raising children today, up from 3.4 million in 1970, according to the U.S. Census Bureau.

In a reversal of how things were when our moms were raising us, a time when working moms were the exception, today 72 percent of U.S. moms work full-time or part-time. Family-friendly employers exist—and *Working Mother* recognizes shining examples each year as the *Working Mother* 100 Best Companies—but flextime and telecommuting are still untested ideas for most employers. We felt a modern-day survival guide would help show women how they could be compassionate moms *and* terrific employees without feeling like they're sinking in a quicksand of demands and competing needs.

When we sat down to map out this guide, we both tapped yet another source—we interviewed our own mothers. Suzanne comes from a long line of working moms: Her great-grandmother ran a dry-goods store. One grandmother taught fourth grade; the other was a physician.

Tracing her mom's working history, Suzanne realized that her mom was something of a pioneer: She took full charge of her career path and customized it to her life. Unlike most female college classmates who graduated, got married, and started families in quick succession, Suzanne's mom graduated and started working, first as a hospital case aide, then later as a legal proofreader and marketing account executive. After she got married and saw kids in her future, she launched a computer dating business, which gave her more control over her time. Once the nest emptied, she went back to school and became a psychoanalyst. So when Suzanne was 10 years old, she already knew she'd work someday. Following her mom's multifaceted career, she figured she'd be a professional ice skater who owned a flower shop and worked as a Lois Lane–type reporter.

Teresa searched for the survival strategy her own mother deployed when she and her dad raised half a dozen kids. She wondered how her mom cooked, cleaned, shopped, served as the troop leader, attended basketball games, and managed to stay awake during band and ballet recitals. How she nursed scraped knees, flu-riddled bodies, and broken hearts; saved for college; and had the sex talk—six times!—while working full-time as a sales rep, then later as an elder-care nurse. Her mom's secret: "I drank a lot of tea." Every one of her children knew that when Mom walked through the door, reports of calamity, requests for money, or questions about what's for dinner had to wait until she had her cup of Tetley.

Today we call that "me time," and this survival guide is loaded with reminders to take care of yourself. We help you embrace imperfection, let go of guilt, and accept help and offer it in return. Taking advantage of shortcuts and tweaking your life when it's not working are what it takes not only to survive, but to thrive. This guide doesn't promise that you'll never again have to take work calls on the weekend, that your kids will suddenly play quietly in the corner, or that raviolis won't occasionally explode. But we hope, in the midst of all that chaos, that the tips in this book will help you remain calm as you speed-dial the pizza place.

Suzanne Riss and Teresa Palagano

What you told us

No one's more of an expert on working moms than, well, a working mom. To tap your collective wisdom, *Working Mother* conducted a survey online from February to March 2011, and 1,053 of you took the time to tell your side of the story. Here's a snapshot of the working moms who participated:

What is your age?

18–24 **1.7%**	40–44 **20.8%**
25–29 **8.5%**	45–49 **12.1%**
30–34 **19.1%**	50+ **14.7%**
35–39 **23.1%**	

What is the highest level of education you have completed?
Some high school **0.9%**
Graduated from high school **8.8%**
Attended college, but did not graduate **23.6%**
Graduated from a four-year college **32.9%**
Post-graduate study without a degree **5.5%**
Master's degree **20.7%**
Doctoral degree **1.6%**
Other professional degree (MD, LLB, etc.) **5.9%**

How many children under the age of 18 do you have?

1 **33.1%**	4 **3.4%**
2 **36.9%**	5+ **1.3%**
3 **12.5%**	My kids are over 18 **12.7%**

What are the ages of your children under 18?

Younger than 1 **9.1%**	10–12 **26%**
1–3 **39.8%**	13–15 **21.1%**
4–6 **42.4%**	16–17 **12.4%**
7–9 **33.2%**	

What is your current marital status?
Married **79%**
Separated/divorced **10.4%**
Single, never married **7.2%**
Cohabiting **2.8%**
Widowed **0.5%**

Which of the following best describes your state of employment?
Employed full-time (30+ hours per week) **62.5%**
Employed part-time (fewer than 30 hours per week) **10.6%**
Not employed: temporarily unemployed **3.8%**
Not employed: student **1.2%**
Not employed: retired **2.8%**
Not employed: homemaker **16.3%**
Other **2.8%**

Are you self-employed? (among employed or temporarily unemployed
respondents)
Yes **10.4%**   No **89.6%**

What is your job title? (among employed respondents)
Manager/administrator **26.6%**
Professional (physician, lawyer, etc.) **23%**
Clerical/administrative **16%**
Corporate officer/senior level executive/owner/partner **8.8%**
Sales **5.5%**
Technical/support service **4.5%**
Other **15.6%**

What is your annual individual income? (among employed
respondents)
Under $20,000 **6%** $75,000–$99,999 **14.4%**
$20,000–$29,999 **7.3%** $100,000–$149,999 **11.8%**
$30,000–$39,999 **10%** $150,000+ **4.9%**
$40,000–$49,999 **11.3%**   Prefer not to answer **11.3%**
$50,000–$74,999 **23%**

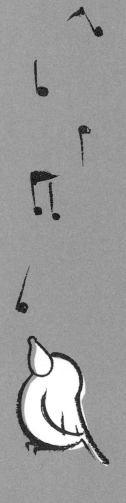

1

Here Comes Baby

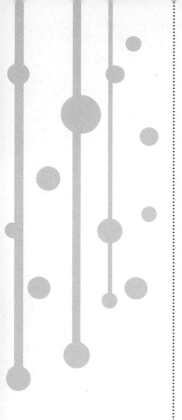

The second you see that plus sign, everything changes—you're going to be a mommy! Talk about overwhelming. And though you have a good nine months to get used to that idea, you have to deal with all the changes pregnancy brings (yikes) while also rocking your job—right now. Double yikes!

Lucky for you, lots of mothers have been down this road before. Here's how to navigate some of the biggest challenges expectant and brand-new working moms face.

Telling your boss

Sharing the happy news with family and friends is the easy part. They'll smile, hug, congratulate you, and maybe even cry. Chances are, sharing the news with your boss and coworkers won't be as heartwarming—they might worry that you won't come back to work or question how committed you are to your job. While you should not feel pressured to tell until you're good and ready, you'll know you've waited too long when they start slipping Weight Watchers brochures in your purse. To get the timing right, follow these guidelines:

Before you go public Read your employer's disability and maternity-leave policies. Labor, as well as prenatal and postpartum care, are often covered as medical disabilities.

8 weeks If you have severe nausea or your pregnancy is high risk, let your boss in on the news early, so that your company can plan ahead in case you need extra time away. Also tell your boss early if your job is physically strenuous or if you need special accommodations, such as cutting back on travel. If you work for yourself, 8 weeks is a good time to start planning out what projects need to be completed before your baby is here and to begin the hunt for someone who can fill in for you while you're on leave. A word of caution for all new moms: It's unrealistic to think that you'll work while the baby naps.

12 weeks Most women tell colleagues they're expecting when the risk of having a miscarriage decreases. About 80 percent of pregnancy loss occurs during the first 12 weeks.

20 weeks If you're resisting revealing your pregnancy, it's at this stage that you'll begin to show a baby bump that can no longer be creatively camouflaged. Not sure if your workplace is family friendly? Well, there's no time like this week to find out.

Getting through the workday

Pregnancy can be a beautiful experience with some not-so-pretty side effects, including varicose veins, gas, bloating, hemorrhoids, acne, and elephant ankles, not to mention unending exhaustion. Growing a new human requires lots of energy and profound physical changes. Pregnancy isn't something you can power through. There's really just one thing you should do: Succumb. How to cope:

Go to bed at least an hour earlier. If you're used to going to sleep around 10 p.m., don't be surprised if you crawl into bed around 8 p.m. Look for napping opportunities throughout the day—even 15 minutes will feel amazing. If you have a door, close it and snooze. Slip out to the parking lot and climb into the back of your car. Scope out an empty conference room— lock the door, shut off the lights.

Eat for stamina. When you want to inhale a pint of Chunky Monkey, resist at least most of the time. The usual good-for-you foods like protein, whole grains, fruits, and vegetables will make a significant difference in your energy level.

(**survey says**)

How far along were you when you told your boss you were pregnant?

36%
Before 12 weeks

55%
13–20 weeks

9%
After 21 weeks

Hydrate. Drink plenty of water—it carries nutrients through the blood to your baby. Staying hydrated lessens the chance of preterm labor and miscarriage, and it can help alleviate nausea.

Exercise. Try to take breaks to stretch and walk, even for 5 to 10 minutes. Prenatal yoga or swimming at lunchtime or after work are good options. Mild exercise can ward off fluid retention, boost energy, and help you sleep better. Plus, working out will help counter that Chunky Monkey habit.

Avoiding nausea

To keep nausea and vomiting at bay, avoid big meals and nosh on snacks throughout the day. Pass on rich, spicy, acidic, or fried foods. Your stomach will thank you. Always have foods that you can tolerate on hand—think almonds or crackers. Experiment with different remedies, even acupressure bracelets, to settle your stomach. At meetings, suck on ginger candies, sip warm ginger tea, or drink ginger ale (the kind with real ginger).

Also, your sense of smell may rival that of a bloodhound—hardly a welcome superpower when a bologna sandwich four cubicles away makes you gag. Because hot foods have stronger aromas, try eating cold or room-temperature food. Also steer clear of stuffy rooms and heavy scents.

Dressing for success

Your first trip to the maternity store may feel like a visit to Mars, but in time you'll be able to locate the granny-panty aisle blindfolded while eating a slice of veggie pizza and texting your sister. You're a working woman, so you'll want to keep looking like your usual polished self. Here's how:

- Use elastic belly bands under your tops to keep your bump from peeking out (and to hold up your pants).

- Invest in a few work essentials in neutral colors that you can mix and match.

Negotiating maternity leave

Pregnancy and delivery are usually treated like any other medical disability, so sick-day and disability rules apply. Once you've given birth or adopted, maternity leave kicks in. Some tactics to try to maximize or extend this time include:

- Simply ask. A full 30 percent of working women participating in the *Working Mother* survey said that they negotiated a longer maternity leave than their companies typically provided.

- Offer to work from home for a period of time when your allotted leave time ends.

- Ask if you can phase back to a full-time schedule by coming in for shorter days or a partial week, such as three days at first, and gradually building back up to full time.

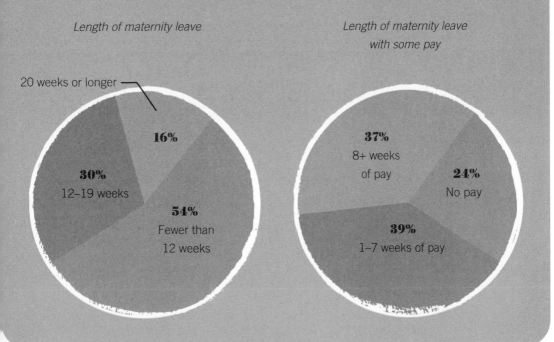

Length of maternity leave

Length of maternity leave with some pay

20 weeks or longer

16%

30%
12–19 weeks

54%
Fewer than
12 weeks

37%
8+ weeks
of pay

24%
No pay

39%
1–7 weeks of pay

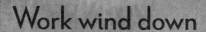

Work wind down

Planning can take a lot of stress out of those crucial weeks before you go on maternity leave. You can adapt this time line to fit your needs:

Now Whether pregnant or adopting, find out how much paid time off you can apply to your maternity leave. Start stockpiling. If you work for yourself, consider how much time you can realistically take off.

20 weeks Make a list of all your responsibilities, both short and long term. Set priorities about what you personally need to do. Start there.

25 weeks Talk to your boss about coverage during your leave. Decide if it makes sense to hire someone or to parcel out tasks to coworkers.

27 weeks Use your list of tasks and recommend the best stand-in for each one. Focus on your highest priorities first.

27 weeks Secure an ally in the office, preferably another mom, who can help you navigate professionally pre- and postpartum.

30 weeks Inform all your business contacts what the plan will be during your leave and whom they should contact in your absence.

31 weeks Gradually start transporting home any personal items you don't want to leave at the office during your time off.

32 weeks Set an official last day and inform all parties. Be sure to tidy up your desk each day when you leave, just in case.

33 weeks Train your replacements and start handing over your tasks, so you'll be around to answer any questions while they learn.

34 weeks Mentally prepare for an office baby shower, which could happen at any time! Write thank-you notes. You won't have time after your baby is born.

- Buy garments that fit well through the shoulders, no matter what size you were before.

- Go for empire-waist tops, dresses, and tunics. You'll be happy to have these for postpartum-wear too. It will also help to have different sizes as you gradually gain weight during pregnancy—and then lose it postpregnancy.

- Accessorize! Colorful scarves, pendant necklaces, and bangle bracelets—not to be worn all at the same time—can make you look glamorous and take the emphasis off your belly.

- Exposing your belly at work is never appropriate; pregnancy is no exception—no matter how adorable that belly is!

Parenting admin

There are a few mandatory administrative tasks for parents-to-be. This type of work is not as fun as picking out nursery colors, but—like filing your tax return—it's the smart thing to do, and you'll feel much better when it's over.

Write a will. In its simplest form, a will is a legal statement that says who your child's legal guardians will be if, heaven forbid, something happens to you and your spouse. Warning: Writing a will can lead to difficult marital conversations—"There's no way your sister is getting the kids. She has that crazy Doberman, and their house smells like cheese!" Be sure to check with your chosen guardians before making it official.

Life insurance. Your employer may include life insurance in your benefits; however, most parents should supplement this with term insurance. Do research and talk to a financial advisor to calculate the best amount of coverage for your family: A common amount for parents is 10 times your yearly salary.

Savings. A traditional savings plan can reduce stress and cover you during emergencies. A general guideline is to set aside

{ mom to mom }

"I thought I'd fit right back into my prepregnancy clothes after the baby was born. Boy, was I wrong."

Foraging for childcare

What type of childcare you pick depends on variables like your child's age, whether you prefer individual care or a group setting, cost, hours, and convenience. This process may be your first experience with maternal instinct—pay attention to your gut feelings, they're valid! Unless you're going with a relative or friend you know well, check references. Use this chart to find the option that feels right to you:

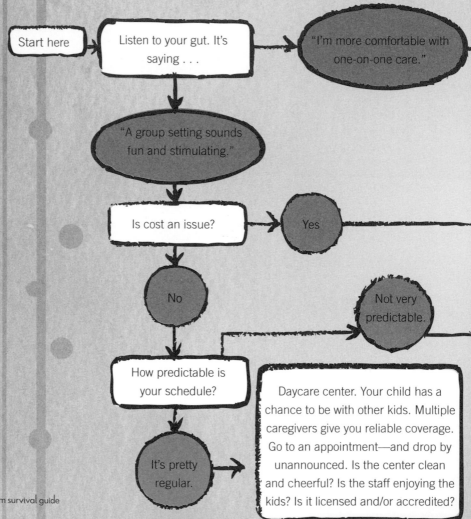

Start here

Listen to your gut. It's saying . . .

"I'm more comfortable with one-on-one care."

"A group setting sounds fun and stimulating."

Is cost an issue?

Yes

No

Not very predictable.

How predictable is your schedule?

It's pretty regular.

Daycare center. Your child has a chance to be with other kids. Multiple caregivers give you reliable coverage. Go to an appointment—and drop by unannounced. Is the center clean and cheerful? Is the staff enjoying the kids? Is it licensed and/or accredited?

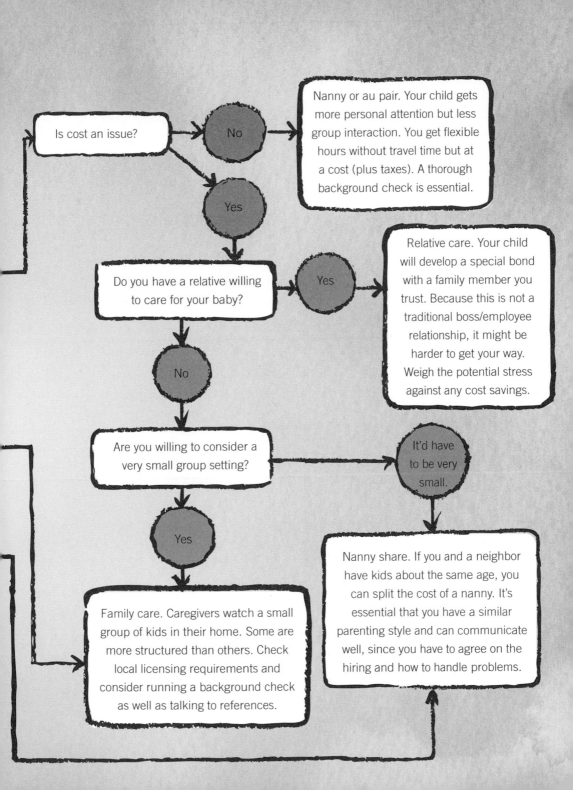

Is cost an issue?

No

Nanny or au pair. Your child gets more personal attention but less group interaction. You get flexible hours without travel time but at a cost (plus taxes). A thorough background check is essential.

Yes

Do you have a relative willing to care for your baby?

Yes

Relative care. Your child will develop a special bond with a family member you trust. Because this is not a traditional boss/employee relationship, it might be harder to get your way. Weigh the potential stress against any cost savings.

No

Are you willing to consider a very small group setting?

It'd have to be very small.

Yes

Family care. Caregivers watch a small group of kids in their home. Some are more structured than others. Check local licensing requirements and consider running a background check as well as talking to references.

Nanny share. If you and a neighbor have kids about the same age, you can split the cost of a nanny. It's essential that you have a similar parenting style and can communicate well, since you have to agree on the hiring and how to handle problems.

Everybody's business

During pregnancy, friends, family, and colleagues can provide much-appreciated support and information. However, also prepare yourself to hear all manner of unsolicited personal blather, regardless of whether it's appropriate, relevant, or useful. Here is some of what you're likely to encounter anywhere from work to the line at Babies "R" Us.

Stories For every birth, there's a story. And for every story, there's a woman who thinks you must hear hers. Some are helpful. Tales of homicidal umbilical cords and newborns who slept 10 minutes a day, however, are not. At the office, protect yourself by avoiding eye contact—and keep moving. Headphones give a signal to leave you alone. If you're cornered, cut it short with a "Thanks for sharing" followed by excusing yourself to use the restroom.

Advice Your mother, mother-in-law, or random aunt didn't have to work while she was pregnant or when she had young kids, so why do you? Um, she also smoked and enjoyed a few G&Ts every afternoon at 4 p.m., but we've progressed since then. Advice can range from fantastic to absurd, so this is when you need to employ your new-mommy filter. Take what you like and leave the rest.

Questions Yeah, yeah, it takes a village and all that, but that doesn't mean the village—especially your boss and coworkers—needs to know how you feel about vaginal delivery. Smother inappropriate queries with a blanket of vague: "We'll see how it turns out," smile, and walk away.

Comments If one more person says it looks like you're having twins, you may explode. The trouble with insensitive comments is that they take you by surprise. To avoid weeping in the office ladies' room, be ready with some snappy comebacks and share the insanity with a close girlfriend, so you can both have a good laugh.

6 months' worth of expenses. Only after you feel comfortable that your emergency fund is adequate and you're maximizing your retirement savings in a tax-free savings vehicle such as a company 401(k), 403(b), or IRA should you get ready to open up a college fund. Yes, you want to save as much for college as you can, but remember: Your child can get a loan to pay for college. You're on your own to pay for retirement.

Fighting fear

You're innocently sitting at your desk when your mind swings from happy baby images to everything that could possibly go wrong. Don't Google those unnerving conditions. Do pick one or two reputable pregnancy books or websites that you can turn to for reliable answers. Rest assured: These dark thoughts are normal for pregnant women. We've been there, and we have two words for you: Let go.

Accept your lack of control. Of course, you will do everything in your power to ensure a healthy baby and a safe delivery. However, you cannot control the birth process any more than you'll be able to control your adventurous toddler.

This free-for-all can be especially frustrating for professional women because it's so different from the work environment where spreadsheets add up, meetings are at certain times, and you can delegate tasks. Oh, and you know what you're doing because you've done it before. If you feel the paranoia creeping in, take a deep breath and a walk outside to clear your head before returning to work.

Address your emotions. If stress is still winning, try putting your fears down in a journal—and out of your head. Education can also lessen stress. Ask your doctor about any fears that relate to your family history, your age, or anything troubling that you read or hear. If worries persist, talk to your physician to rule out prenatal anxiety or depression. Keep in mind that the majority of pregnancies go smoothly.

Back-to-work countdown

4 weeks Line up your childcare arrangements. Know what the plan will be, then secure backup care and backup, backup care.

3 weeks Check your post-baby wardrobe. See if some of your maternity wear would work (nothing too big or stained or that makes you feel dowdy), whether you can borrow some items from a friend, or if you need to buy some basics to help you through until your body is back to its fighting weight. Make sure you have a bra that fits well. Stock up on bra pads and invest in a separate breast pump for the office if you plan to pump there.

2 weeks Call your ally at the office for an update. This way you won't feel blindsided the day you return to work. You can have this conversation in person if you drop by the office for a short visit so everyone can meet your baby.

1 week Try a couple of trial runs. Have your caregiver stop by, or drop off your baby at daycare for a couple hours, while you go out for a cup of coffee or to run errands. This will give you time away from your baby, help you adjust to the new-mom changes (like how long it takes to get out the door), and give you an opportunity to go over any requests with your caregiver. Feel free to drop back in unexpectedly to see how everything's going.

After baby: Maternity leave

If you've imagined your maternity leave as a sabbatical—a time to grow herbs, reorganize the home office, maybe even take Italian lessons—you will be disappointed. Yes, newborns sleep 16 to 20 hours a day. The catch is: they're not sleeping that many hours in a row. Expect to be feeding, burping, changing, swaddling, and rocking your newborn around the clock, leaving you with little time or energy for anything but catnaps. Say "arrivederci" to Italian lessons; you'll be lucky if you can process how to screw the top back on to the toothpaste.

Isolation

Aside from being on call 24/7 and feeling utterly overwhelmed, isolation can be a big problem, especially if you're used to a busy office. In our survey, 28 percent of working moms reported feeling isolated, and 37 percent said they did not have enough support and help during maternity leave. Some strategies for surviving the deserted island of new motherhood:

Connect with new moms. Join a new-moms group so that you have a network of women sharing similar experiences. Using them as sounding boards—even for middle-of-the-night e-mails about the colors of normal poop—will help you feel less alone.

Get outside. Start the day by putting your baby in a stroller or a sling and going for a walk. Exposure to daylight will help your baby learn the difference between day and night, and the exercise and fresh air will rejuvenate you.

Keep up. Even though you may not care what's going on in the world, glance at the news every few days. This will help you feel less like a cavewoman, especially when you return to work.

Jonesing for the office

Obsessively checking company e-mail, panicking when your BlackBerry is out of reach, and calling coworkers to see what you're missing is no formula for a peaceful maternity leave.

How often did you stay in
touch with the office while
on maternity leave?

47%
A couple of times

26%
Weekly or a couple of
times a week

22%
Not at all

5%
Daily

The following steps will help you focus on mommy-and-me classes rather than missed meetings.

- When your baby is born, ask a family member to contact your office ally with the news to disseminate at work. And once the baby is home, follow up with pictures.

- Ask your ally to contact you only if any major changes occur. These do not include rumors of office affairs, a new cafeteria menu, or schadenfreude that Amy in accounts payable has gained 10 pounds and, girl, you should see what she's squeezing into these days.

- If withdrawal symptoms are severe, don't call or visit your office; watch a few episodes of *The Office* and you'll realize you're not missing a thing.

Will I really return to work?

When you were planning your maternity leave, you were confident that you'd go back to work. But now you're on the fence. In our survey, two out of five working moms said that they struggled with this question. If you're one of the fortunate few who have the financial resources to consider opting out of the workforce for a while, here's what to think about:

Can I afford to take time off? Do the math. How much will childcare, commuting, lunches, and other work-related costs total? How does the family budget look without your income?

How will my career be affected? Talk to other moms who have been there. How much will time off affect your advancement? Your earnings? If you're struggling with financial questions, *The Feminine Mistake: Are We Giving Up Too Much?* by Leslie Bennetts looks at the economics of women quitting their jobs.

How flexible is my employer? If you're not ready to go back, ask if your employer will extend your leave. Three months with your newborn may not be enough time, but six months could do the trick. Or maybe you're ready to return now, but need a transition period or schedule change. Is it possible to ease back in by working part time or from home some days?

What's right for my family? In the end, it's your decision whether returning to work or making a career change that better meshes with your new family—such as going freelance or opening your own business—will be the right decision for you. Remember that mommy intuition we talked about? What's it telling you? Listen.

Enjoy yourself now

There's a saying about parenthood: The days are long, and the years are short. Being a new mom can be exhausting and frustrating, but it's also a truly precious time. You will be constantly amazed by your baby: How she gazes at you when you feed her; the first time she smiles her real smile; the moment you try to tape on the newborn diapers only to discover they're now too tight (didn't they just fit last night?!). You will also be amazed by your partner: How achingly sweet it is to watch your fellow parent and baby together; how much you both talk about poop; how you call each other at least three times a day to exchange updates on your little one.

Your time off is a gift. It's your chance to focus on nothing else except figuring out how to be a family. It's also the time for the old you to make friends with the new you. Up until now, much of your identity probably has been tied tightly to your career and what you've achieved. Now you've got an entirely new, and absolutely huge, change to your job description: Mom.

We're not going to say nothing will change at work. Chances are things *will* change—and probably because you want them to. Your priorities might shift a bit, and that's perfectly okay. You may need some trial and error to figure out how to be the working mom you want to be. And that's perfectly okay too.

{ mom to mom }

"Going back to work was easier than I expected. Since becoming a mom, I've become a better employee. Because I know I have a set amount of time to get everything done before I need to go pick up my child from daycare, I'm more focused, better organized, and more productive."

2

Back to Work

Time to go back to work. Do you feel guilty, elated, uncertain? The polar opposite of how you thought you would feel? Take a deep breath and remember that more than half of all new moms go back to work when their infants are younger than 1 year old—many with conflicted emotions.

Hard to focus on profit-and-loss statements when your little miracle is at home? Even those of us who skip with joy back to the bosom of business—where we look forward to daily lunch breaks, intellectual stimulation, and adult conversation—may still experience less-than-inspiring moments of doubt and frustration. The good news is, despite inevitable ups and downs, things will get easier. Try these strategies to help you get through those first weeks.

- Accept that you may have to "fake it 'til you make it." Have ready a short positive answer to "How are you?" along the lines of "It's good to be back."

- Give yourself a break. Expect at least the first month to be challenging and don't beat yourself up. Call your partner or a friend if you need to hear a supportive voice.

- Remember that you're doing what's best for you and your family, and that you're helping to give your baby the very best life possible.

- Think about the example you're setting—a financially independent woman with a career and aspirations.

- Cherish the amazing feeling at the end of the day when you get to see your child again.

Handling separation anxiety — your own

For all the talk about a baby's separation anxiety, the teary red face and the outstretched arms will likely belong to you. In the *Working Mother* survey, 67 percent of the working moms we surveyed experienced separation anxiety when they first returned to work. Your baby will be fine; it might take a while for you to adjust. Once you see that your baby is happy and thriving, your own emotions will stabilize. Here are some tips to ease your anxiety:

- Place a photo of your baby on your desk. Ask your caregiver to occasionally take and e-mail photos.

- Keep in mind that babies usually have no trouble staying with a childcare provider during the day as long as they're being fed, changed, and treated with love. This doesn't mean that you're being replaced—it means that there are more people in your child's life to love and care for her.

- Know that there's no scientific evidence that suggests that children are harmed when their mothers work outside the home. The American Academy of Pediatrics reports that a child who is emotionally well adjusted, well loved, and well cared for will thrive regardless of whether his mother works outside the home.

When things don't get better

Postpartum depression can come at any time during your baby's first year—it affects one out of every five new moms. Diagnosing it can be difficult because symptoms, like mood swings and fatigue, are common postpartum. If you experience excessive sadness or guilt, a change in appetite, insomnia, anxiety, irritability, or you just don't **feel** right, call your doctor right away. It's important for you (and your baby) to get help.

{ mom to mom }

"When I was younger, I stressed about having my three boys in daycare while I worked as an engineer. I can now say all my boys are in college and each has a good head on his shoulders."

Keeping tabs on baby

Whether your infant is at a childcare center or one-on-one with a nanny, you will want to know what your baby is doing while you're at work. Make it clear when your caregiver should call, for example, if your baby isn't feeling well, is crying uncontrollably, or gets hurt. You can also set up one or two appointed times to check in. Refrain from calling once an hour on the hour—this does no one any good.

Don't ask your caregiver to videochat or submit detailed reports throughout the day on your baby's every move. Her top priority is to focus on your child. Ask her to track things such as the number of diaper changes, feedings, and naps. If possible, build time into both your and your nanny's schedules to review the day's happenings.

Another no-no—surveillance. A spy cam in the baby's nursery? If you feel an overwhelming urge to go all high-tech on the babysitter, reconsider your choice. Your peace of mind will depend on your comfort level with the person caring for your baby. If you don't feel at ease, find someone you can trust.

Mother's intuition can be subtle, and you may not recognize it the first time it taps you on the shoulder. If you're feeling uncomfortable about anything relating to your baby, such as behavior or developmental issues, speak up to your partner, your baby's pediatrician, or a mommy friend. Once you're tuned in to your gut, you'll be amazed at what it can tell you.

Guilty as charged?

You will probably also discover a new level of guilt. Two-thirds of the working moms in our survey said they feel guilty about being away from their children when at work. As a mom, you can feel guilty over anything from not making your own organic baby food to secretly loving the solitude of your cubicle. When you're home, you will think about work and vice versa—which will make you feel guilty. Feeling

Time for childcare

When you're a working mom, the need for childcare is a given. Which option you choose, however, is totally up to you. Curious what other moms are doing? Here's what the moms in our survey who use childcare told us:

On average, how many hours per week do you have childcare?

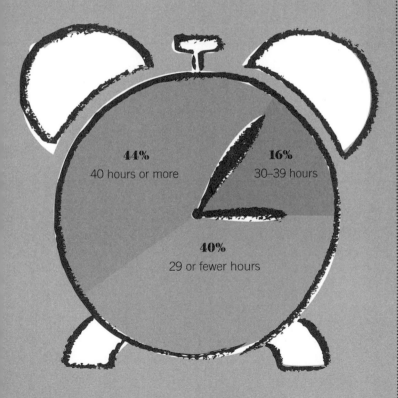

44%
40 hours or more

16%
30–39 hours

40%
29 or fewer hours

Which types of childcare do you use?

45%
Childcare center, full time

27%
Parent or relative

19%
Part-time caregiver, mother's helper, or occasional babysitter

17%
Full-time caregiver

14.5%
Childcare center, part time

Pump it up: Moms' tips

Working moms with babies often have a new companion—the pump. In our survey, we asked veteran moms for their top tips. From "drink lots of water" to "stick with it," here's some in-the-trenches advice:

What you need

"Don't cheap out on a breast pump. Buy the best you can afford."

"Keep a pump at home and another one at work. This will eliminate schlepping and stop panic when you forget it due to mommy brain."

"At work, double up on the pump parts that need to be washed. That way, when you're in a rush, you'll have backups for your next session."

"Buy a hands-free pumping bustier. It may seem silly until you realize you can pump and balance your checkbook at the same time. Genius."

"Keep an extra bra, blouse, and breast pads in your office for leaks."

> "Be patient and committed. You'll do fine."

Preparing to pump

Get to know your pump while you're still on maternity leave. Adjust the dates if you have a longer leave. Note: If you're breastfeeding a child under the age of 1 and work for a company

Before baby's born

Buy a pump or two and extra parts (see above). Consider a hands-free model. Open the box, and examine and wash the parts. Read all of the instructions.

2 weeks after baby's born

Pump once a day in the morning when you're likely to produce more milk, and include your partner in a feeding. Try different bottles and nipples if necessary.

Baby is 1 month old

Optional: Pump a few times a day and freeze the milk to build up your supply for when you go back to work. Date and double-bag milk before freezing. Use the oldest first.

Helpful hints

"Ask ahead of time for an arrangement if your company doesn't have a lactation room and you don't have an office."

"Be committed. Aggressively protect pumping time by blocking it off on your schedule."

"A discreet note helps keep people from barging into your office."

"Pump as soon as you get to work. In the morning you'll have more milk and you'll be less likely to put it off once you're involved in a project."

"No matter how busy your day gets, don't let yourself become engorged. This puts you at high risk for mastitis."

"Keep photos of your baby in your pumping bag to help stimulate milk production. Or watch a video of your baby on your phone."

"Consider learning how to hand express milk. In a dire emergency, you can do this in a restroom to relieve pressure until you can pump."

"Accidents will happen. Laugh them off."

"Relax. Stressing out makes it all the more difficult."

with more than 50 employees, U.S. law requires your employer to provide a private lactation room, and it can't be the ladies' room.

Before you go back to work	You're back at work	Any time
Go over the procedures for breastmilk storage, thawing, and feeding with your baby's caregiver. Set up a system for your caregiver to record the ounces your baby eats.	Track the number of ounces you pump daily. Keep up with how much your baby eats, but don't stress if you need to supplement with formula. Any amount of breastmilk is good.	Your body can adjust to a new feeding or pumping schedule. Gradually reduce pumping sessions, but still maintain a basic schedule such as nursing before and after work.

On the bright side

A day in the life of a working mom isn't easy, but here's how to see the best side of some bleak scenarios:

When None of your work clothes fit—even the ones reserved for PMS bloat.

Tell yourself You *will* eventually fit into them again, but for now a girl's gotta wear something. Time to shop!

When Your leaky breasts leave you with two bull's-eyes on your blouse after a conference call gone bad.

Tell yourself Your next pumping session is sure to yield a new record! High five!

When You're not there on Tuesday, when your baby eats pureed peas for the first time.

Tell yourself You'll be there on Saturday morning to give him his first taste of pureed squash. Yum!

When Chronic mommy guilt has convinced you that Baby Lindsay will need therapy before she's three.

Tell yourself Lindsay will have a leg up on her peers since they probably won't find their first psychologist until their early twenties.

When Your new zero-tolerance for bull has you rolling your eyes at your boss and hanging up on clients.

Tell yourself At least now everyone knows exactly how you feel.

When You're running on yet another night of no sleep and doze off during the weekly budget meeting.

Tell yourself Everyone deserves at least 10 minutes of sheer heaven.

When After a full day of work you are—big surprise—too tired for sex.

Tell yourself You have a chance to catch up on your sleep.

guilty, however, saps emotional energy that could be deployed elsewhere. Here's how to ease your conscience:

Ask "Why?" Try to figure out what exactly is triggering the guilt. Are you worried that you're not as good as other moms? That maybe you don't know what's best for your baby? When those intrusive thoughts pop up, it can help to have a little mantra, something like, "I'm the best mom for *my* baby." It may feel a little cheesy at first, but soon enough those words will turn into belief, and belief will turn into confidence.

Stand your ground. If another person is making you feel guilty, stand up for yourself. If your mom thinks you should make a home-cooked meal by 6 p.m. daily—you know, the way she did—acknowledge that those dinners were great and remind her that your life is different and your family is okay with that.

Forgive yourself. You may feel conflicted that you should have done something and didn't, like reading to your baby, or that you did something you shouldn't have, like yelling at your partner. Make peace with the fact that you're not perfect, apologize when it's appropriate, and try to do better next time.

Don't go there. Guilt will still seep through the most solid defenses. Simply being aware of it can help you let it go. Also try your favorite stress relievers—do a yoga podcast, knit, say a prayer, sing to your baby, talk to a friend. If an overdose of guilt is making you feel depressed or anxious, or eat or drink excessively, talk to your doctor right away.

Back on track
Like Grandma said, much of life is simply getting through the rough parts. While she may not have had pressure from her boss to come back to work early or pump breastmilk on cue, it's clear that woman was wise. Going back to work after maternity leave can be rough indeed, but smooth sailing is on the horizon . . . when your kids graduate from college.

"Do not feel guilty for supporting yourself and your family by working or pursuing a career. You are setting an example for your children that is invaluable."

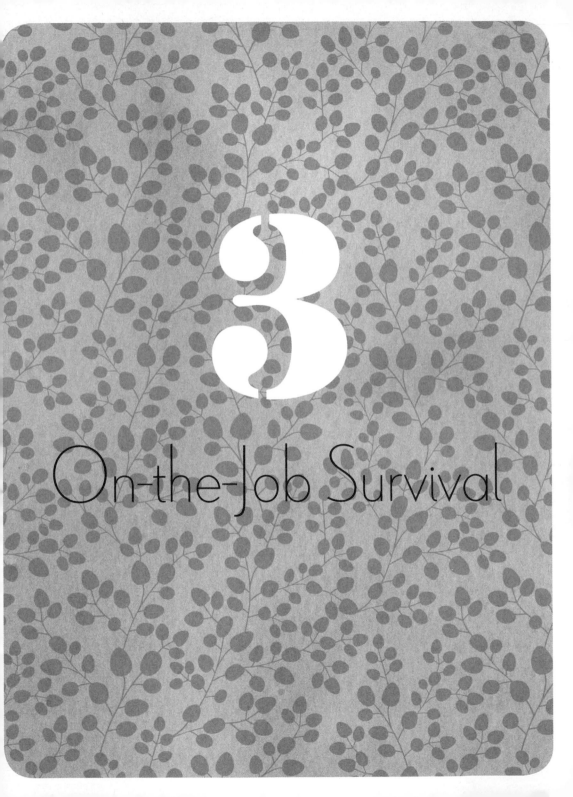

3

On-the-Job Survival

Picture this—your husband's knee surgery coincides with your big sales presentation. Both land on the first day of school, during which Junior develops a severe case of separation anxiety and you get your period four days early. Worst-case scenario or just another day in the life of a working mom?

While it's impossible to anticipate every problem you'll experience as a working mom, there are a few common ones that are very likely to come up on the battlefield. Being smart and cautious around these land mines is what separates the working women from the working girls. Do you have what it takes to survive and thrive as a mom with a full-time job? Of course you do! Here's the intel you need to know.

Handling a last-minute meeting

Your boss calls an urgent 5:30 p.m. meeting, the exact time that you're supposed to relieve the sitter. You don't want to look like a clock-watcher or miss crucial after-hours meetings, so prepare as best you can for short-notice gatherings. Keep in mind, it's a two-way street: You want to leave work at the last minute when your baby spikes a fever, so it makes sense to stay late if you can when your boss asks you.

Make preemptive strikes by discussing this scenario with your boss, spouse, and daycare provider ahead of time. Talk to your partner about what you'll do when whoever is planning to pick up the baby can't do it and what to do if you both can't make it. Try to keep in touch during the day—it's safe to assume that either of you could get tripped up at the last minute. If you have a nanny, talk in advance about those cases when both you and your partner are late. Could she stay late in exchange for a prenegotiated after-hours rate? Or take your child to a neighbor to wait for you? To be fair to your nanny, if you're often late, adjust the hours. If your child is at a daycare center, know the late policy, which often involves a hefty fee. Consider arranging a backup plan with another child's parents in case something unexpected pops up for any of you.

Still no luck? Call for reinforcements from Team Backup. All working moms must have people to cover in the case of a crisis. Your Team B could include friends, neighbors, stay-at-home moms, and other working moms. Reciprocate proactively by making it a point to do your allies favors when you can, not only when they're in crisis mode.

When you simply can't get a backup, determine if you *must* attend the meeting. Could someone take notes and fill you in later? Could this meeting take place first thing in the morning? Could you call in from home? Don't be afraid to ask if there's a way to make this meeting work without rearranging your caregiving responsibilities.

Staying awake in a meeting

Working moms don't get enough sleep and working moms with a sick kid often don't get any sleep. At times, staying awake at work will be a sheer act of will, especially during endless meetings with speakers filibustering on office supplies and cost containment. Some tips for staying wide-eyed:

Prep. Ten minutes before the meeting, drink a glass of water, eat a handful of nuts, and stretch. If you haven't been mainlining coffee all day, a small hit of caffeine can help.

Don't slump. Sit up straight with shoulders back and feet on the floor. An uncomfortable position makes it harder for you to doze off. If you get too comfortable, you'll soon be snoring.

Get the blood flowing. Do leg lifts under the table. Squeeze a hand exercise ball. Get your heart pumping, but don't go too far. Jogging in place will cause all the other bored-out-of-their-mind attendees to focus on you, not the speaker.

Drink. Bring a big glass of water and drink it—also an excuse for frequent bathroom breaks.

Pinch yourself. If you start to nod off, pull your hair, pinch yourself, or poke yourself with a pen. Pain will bring you back.

Getting out of a client meeting

Depending on your line of work, you may have lots of after-hours meetings and events. Because you know they will happen, and usually at the worst possible time, be prepared to side-step the less crucial ones.

If you know the client well, simply say that you have to get home and offer to have lunch the next day instead. "I'm so sorry, I have a conflict" is a perfectly acceptable excuse. There is no need to overshare about the details of your marriage, your child's health, or your nanny's personal life. State your case with a definitive tone and keep it brief.

Still, there will be that last-minute "I need you to stay as late as it takes to get this done" request that you cannot refuse. If there's no room for flexibility, see if a colleague can join you and excuse yourself early. If you're backed into a corner and your partner can't cover the kids, speed-dial your backups.

Have rations on hand

We've done it—raided our kids' Halloween basket for breakfast, choked down leftover pizza for three lunches in a row, gone several days without a single glass of water. Eating well when you're eating on the run requires strategy. Plan healthy meals and snacks to prevent indulging in morning-meeting muffins, potato chip lunches, and afternoon vending-machine runs.

Five ways to sneak out of a meeting

We've all had the experience of too many meetings keeping us from getting our real work done. Playing hooky from group gatherings sometimes is a necessity to stay sane. What to do:

1 **Delegate.** Ask a member of your team to take notes for you during the portion of the meeting that you miss. Follow up by letting your boss or client know that you're up to speed.

2 **Plan your escape.** Before the meeting starts, tell the group that you unfortunately need to leave early. No need to explain further since you're cutting out to do actual work.

3 **Establish your presence.** Make an insightful or clever comment at the start of the meeting so that others remember that you were, in fact, in attendance.

4 **Position yourself strategically.** Scope out the room and sit where you can make your escape as nonchalantly and quietly (be wary of squeaky chairs) as possible.

5 **Skip excuses.** Have a brief, noncommittal answer, such as "I had a deadline," ready in case anyone questions why you made an early exit. No need to go into details.

Ten steps to get what you want

In the *Working Mother* survey, 64 percent of working moms said they are good at negotiating at work to get what they want. Whether you want flextime or a raise, there's an art to negotiating.

1 **Prepare.** Do your homework so that you know what's happened in similar situations. Talk to other working moms who have what you want and find out how they did it. These women are likely self-motivated and have a track record of dependability—like you!

2 **Let them speak first.** If possible, especially when it comes to salary negotiations, let the other side talk before you do. Lawyers and mediators say that if you speak first, you're generally at a disadvantage because you risk selling yourself short.

3 **Write it down.** If you're going for flextime, write out how it will up your productivity and explain how you'll keep your boss informed of progress with a short daily e-mail. Having a written proposal that outlines when others can expect to see completed projects will help clarify the parameters and take the burden off your boss.

4 **Be confident.** It's a myth that women are weaker negotiators than men. However, women do seem to lack confidence more often than men do. No one can read your mind—you need to ask for what you want. Be clear and direct, and look them in the eye.

5 **Know your numbers.** Anticipate what the other person will want. If you're asking for more money, cushion your numbers to leave some room for negotiation. Caveat: Be realistic about your request. Overinflated numbers could undermine your credibility.

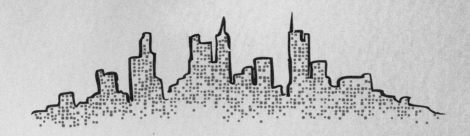

6 **Emphasize the benefits.** Regardless of what you're asking for, focus on what's in it for them. For example, telecommuting may help the company reduce overhead costs and allow you to communicate more easily with customers in other time zones.

7 **Listen!** The more you can get the other side to open up, the more likely you'll find a creative solution. You don't need to decide on the spot. If you reach a stalemate, table the discussion. Note what you talked about so you can pick up right where you left off.

8 **Connect and keep cool.** Find some common ground and mind your manners. It's possible to be nice and courteous while remaining firm about your request. People are more likely to do things for you if they like you.

9 **Propose a trial run.** Offer a trial period, such as working from home one day per week for a month, after which your manager can evaluate if it's working. A boss who has an out clause will feel more relaxed about giving the experiment a chance.

10 **Have a plan B.** If you can't get flextime, ask for more vacation or to leave early on Fridays. Negotiating is about giving the other person the illusion of control, like the tactics you use with your toddler: "Which would you like: peas or carrots? You choose."

If I knew then . . .

Got a secret weapon to get you through rough patches? Top picks:

52% A helpful partner

47% Lowering expectations

29% Help from friends and family

22% An understanding boss

6% Lots of hired help

In our survey, working moms listed advice that they wish they had heard much earlier. Here are their top mom-to-mom tips:

● "Make time for yourself."

● "If momma ain't happy, nobody is happy. So figure out what you need to be happy."

● "Accept good enough."

● "Build a network of support."

● "Learn that you can't do everything."

● "Tell your kids you love them and hug them as often as possible."

● "Be careful not to overcommit."

● "Stay focused. You'll get everything done faster."

● "Leave work at work."

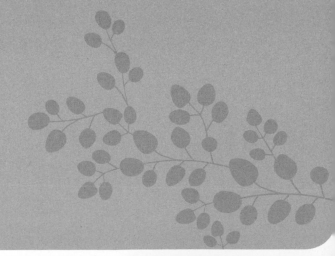

Stock up. Put yourself on the family grocery list so your work food isn't an afterthought. Buy healthy, shelf-stable items that can live in your desk drawer or in the office freezer, like cans of soup, frozen prepared meals, instant oatmeal, nuts, and crackers. If you're up for it, use Sundays as a day to prepare soups, hard-boiled eggs, or even PB&J sandwiches that you can store in the freezer until you need them. Keep a stash of your favorite herbal teas and a bowl of fruit at your desk. No need to muddle through with the office-supplied dregs!

Thwart fridge raiders. Every office has a lunch thief who forages for food in the fridge. Usually it's an underpaid intern who is sick of eating ramen noodles. Protect your lunch by packing it in a brown paper bag, writing your name on it in huge letters, and stapling it shut.

Beware of temptation. If your office has lots of birthday cakes, look-who-just-got-promoted cookies, and thank-you chocolates from clients, resist these empty-calorie minefields. If you get sleepy and crave sugar every day at 3:30 p.m., set an alarm at 3:15 p.m. and have an apple or a cup of tea instead. Who has time to shop for larger clothes or schedule extra training sessions at the gym?

When you screw up

Mistakes happen. Especially when you're overscheduled and exhausted. If your boss is furious because you're late again, missed a meeting, or plain forgot to file the Smithson proposal—you've got to own it. Don't offer a barrage of excuses or blame. Acknowledge that you made a mistake and then fix it to the best of your ability.

You may need to shift around or share some of your family responsibilities so that you can refocus on your career for awhile. If there's a legitimate reason why you've been off your game, consider sharing this with your boss, but only in the context of how you are now going to correct the situation.

{ **mom to mom** }

"I'm not exactly thrilled with my reliance on convenience foods, but thank God for Trader Joe's!"

Best time to ask your boss for a favor

Little Ashley's spring break is coming up and you've promised her Disney this year. It also coincides with your mandatory corporate retreat. What's a working mom to do? Timing is everything, and this is particularly true when trying to get your boss to do something you want. Pick the time you walk into her office wisely. The best times are:

When you haven't asked for anything in a while. Be careful how frequently you ask for special treatment. An overly needy employee can start to sound like white noise.

After you've said yes. If your manager asks you to work late, travel, or take an appointment in her place, do it whenever possible. Agreeing to her request will make her more likely to agree to yours.

When you're in rock-star mode. Did you just finish a report that's getting glowing reviews? Did you sign on a highly sought-after client? If you've recently done something awesome for the company, your boss is more likely to reward your contribution.

When your boss is in a good mood. Is she singing in the office after a romantic weekend? Pick a time when she's happy—not when she's in a big rush or under major stress. If you approach her office and hear shouting, step away from the door.

In advance. No one likes to be put on the spot. If you're asking for time off, do it as far in advance as you can. Note school events and breaks in your work calendar. It doesn't mean that you'll be available for all of them, but it gives you a fighting chance to avoid conflicts.

Managing a boss who isn't a parent

Managers who don't have kids can forget that there's a world outside the office walls. Handle a boss who eats and breathes work with care. Your request to leave in the middle of the day to attend a third-grade performance of "A Day at the Zoo" may be met with a bewildered stare. He can't necessarily appreciate how cute your little lions are or know how much lion cubs cry when they don't see their mommy in the audience.

- Be visible in times of anticipated need. If Thursday night is always a crunch because the budget is due on Friday, stay late or work after your kids are in bed. Being proactive will engender goodwill for the times you can't work after hours.

- Pounce on any mention of non-work-related topics. Does your boss love to run marathons? Encourage your boss to go for a run while you handle things at the office.

- Ask about your boss's family and pets. Your boss may start to see a connection between taking Wolfie, the Siberian husky, to the trainer and taking your son to clarinet lessons.

- Know your audience. If your office is not big on kids, resist the temptation to cover your desk with photos of your kids and their artwork. Instead, limit yourself to one photo and one masterpiece—feel free to rotate them frequently.

Survive and thrive

There's no doubt that surviving and thriving as a working mother requires lots of practice and occasionally some stealth. Being armed to confront the problems that come your way will help you stand tall and find your stride. In fact, as the months and years pass, your problem-solving skills will silently sharpen until one day you're hit with a perfect storm of nightmare situations that you diffuse in, oh, about 15 minutes flat. You won't even think too much about it because you already know what to do without breaking a sweat.

{ mom to mom }

"Don't ever apologize for being a mom or putting your family first."

4

Strategic Alliances

No one knows better than a working mom how complicated life can be (and if you happen to be a single working mom, well, you can multiply the complication factor by at least two). But you can make things a lot easier on yourself and your kids by asking for help when you need it. The catch?

You need to have a network of reliables you can call upon! If you don't already have fellow parents, neighbors, friends, and coworkers you can rely on, it's time do some relationship building. It's actually easier than it sounds: Mrs. Jones next door would probably love a few double-chocolate brownies, and since you made 250 of them, without nuts of course, for the bake sale, there's plenty to spare.

Back up your backups

To avoid the scramble of searching for someone to watch your child last-minute when your usual backups aren't available, keep a list of people who might be able pinch hit when Gram's got poker night and your partner's out of town. Zero in on:

Daycare or school staffers They're already cleared as reliable, and often eager for extra cash.

Activity folks Coaches, tutors, and fellow parents from your child's activity circle may be sympathetic to your plight.

Babysitters Contact sitters who are old enough to drive and will follow your safety rules, like making sure everyone buckles up—every time!

Make favor-bank deposits

Giving of yourself, when you can, is currency that can prove invaluable when you're in a jam. It will minimize the guilt and give you more options to choose from when it's your turn to ask for help. Warning: Add to your favor bank only when you feel able. Overextending yourself only leads to exhaustion.

At home Once in a while, pull extra duty on the weekends. Carpool both ways for soccer practice. Host playdates at your house. Text friends when you're at the grocery store or Target and ask if they need anything. Take a group of kids to a baseball game. In general, give other parents a break.

At work Volunteer for some assignments that nobody wants. Cover for a coworker who has to leave to handle a family issue. Compliment the people you work with for a job well done, be proactive about problem solving, and share the credit on projects you lead. Building goodwill with fellow staffers means they'll be more likely to have your back when it counts.

In your community With kids in tow, make some time for those in need—pitch in at a food bank, check on elderly neighbors, attend the firefighters' pancake breakfasts. When you can, offer your skills. Lend marketing expertise to a fundraiser, plant at a city garden, teach a kids' yoga class. Karma is a powerful thing.

Connect with coworkers

Working moms should seek out support wherever they can find it and some of the best sources are, you guessed it, other working moms. Hooking up with them can help you get the inside scoop on maternity leave, flextime, working from home, and more. Plus, they're the ones most likely to step up for you, no questions asked, when you have to cope with a family crisis.

Once you've got your allies assembled, it's crucial to keep an eye on your foes and do what you can to steer clear. A common personality: the (usually child-free) coworker who sneers when

{ **mom to mom** }

"When times get crazy, I'm lucky to be able to call on my fully devoted parents, who can't have enough time with my child. Everyone wins!"

When only you will do

Even though you plot every minute of your vacation and personal days with the precision of a surgeon, we recommend keeping some days in reserve for the unexpected. You or your partner must take off from work when:

Your child is sick. If your child is running a temperature, vomiting, or has anything that might be contagious, you can't expose a caregiver or other kids to the risk of getting sick. If your child is sick, go to the pediatrician. The earlier you get a prognosis, the faster you can figure out a recovery strategy. Can you work from home? Can you split the day with your partner so you can each go to work for half? Know what you're up against so you can figure out a plan.

You're sick. Children in school are little Petri dishes full of every bug out there. All of the hand washing and vitamin C in the world can't stop the occasional bug from getting through. So the same rules apply to you: Don't try to power through the day with cold meds and cough drops. Studies show that employees who take time off when ill use fewer sick days than those who attempt to work when ill. Take the day to recover; your coworkers will thank you for it.

Your child is performing or getting an award. Whether your son is the star of the school play or a caterpillar in the chorus, move heaven and earth to get there. In fact, go early and stay for the post-show lemonade and cookies. Kids need to see Mommy in the audience, but even more, moms need to be there.

you leave work early. There's usually one in every office—the clock-watcher, the martyr who feels that she works harder and longer than everyone else, or the busybody who makes snide comments about everyone. If you feel that others resent that you spend fewer hours in the office, go on the offensive:

- Tout your accomplishments. Bragging about what you do well—without it sounding like bragging—is a key skill.

- Make your schedule known. If you must leave at a certain time every day, do so consistently so no one thinks it's "optional." Luckily, 71 percent of the moms in the *Working Mother* survey said their office is good about scheduling meetings around after-work pickups.

- Stand proud. Never feel ashamed or apologetic for your different hours. Your schedule and performance are between you and your boss, no explanations necessary.

"Help! He loves the babysitter more than me!"

Picture this: You can't wait to get through the door to scoop up your little pumpkin. As soon as he sees you, he not only clings to the sitter but also yells "No!" to you. Sound familiar? Outside of your family, the caregiver is probably the most important person in your network, and nearly one-third of the moms we surveyed said they have felt jealous of that person.

One of the best ways to cope is to congratulate yourself on finding the right person for your child. Your child's bonds with others will never dilute his love for you. In fact, having good relationships with caregivers helps lead to other healthy relationships in his life. Your babysitter is one more person who loves your child. The next step: Reserve activities for you and your child. Maybe it's breakfast, bath time, or bedtime reading. Knowing there's something special that just the two of you share will help get you through those moments when you feel less important or replaced by another.

"Don't say yes to everything that's asked of you."

Nurture your love life

Research tells us that modern-day dads help out much more than our fathers did. Ninety-three percent of the coupled-up working moms we surveyed said that they have a supportive partner at home. (Some working moms also shared with us that they have sex with their partner to relieve stress.) Unfortunately, as a whole, moms still do the majority of chores and childcare despite the fact that there are more mothers in the workforce than ever before. Knowing that you can rely on your partner will help keep your stress level in check and bring the two of you closer, which makes everything feel more manageable. Here are tips for working together:

Divvy up duties. When deciding who does what around the house, match the task with preference, skill, and availability. The spouse who gets home first makes dinner. Include the kids in this equation too, based on their age and abilities. For example, have them empty the dishwasher, make the salad, put out bread, and set and clear the table. Those are a few more things off of your plate, and you're fostering their independence to boot.

Embrace diversity. Step back and resist the urge to supervise, assist, or correct the way your partner does tasks.

Say please and thank you. We know you're an adult. You know these things. But when you're at home, with your people, it's oh-so-easy to forget. Have your children say thank you to whomever provided the meal before they ask to be excused from the table. An attitude of gratitude, kindness, and appreciation is contagious, no matter how small the task.

Talk every day. Have a regular time together after the kids are in bed. Help your kids stick to their bedtime so you aren't getting them water and reading them "just one more" story until it's practically your bedtime. This way you and your partner can unwind together, whether you chat about your days, read the newspaper, or watch reality TV.

Throw down a blanket. Your dates may not be like they used to be—with lots of time to primp and, um, shave your legs. But that's okay. Aim for at least once a month when you and your partner hire a babysitter and get out of the house. Try to avoid falling into a "dinner and a movie" routine. Research shows that novelty—hitting an outdoor concert, theme park, or hiking trail—enhances relationships.

Steal away. It can be difficult for some parents to imagine being apart from the kids for more than a few hours, but the break can be restorative for all. Your escape doesn't have to be elaborate. A bed-and-breakfast an hour away could do the trick. And if you can't get away, arrange for the kids to have a sleepover with friends, then return the favor when the friends' parents want an escape.

Do what works for you. While we strongly encourage you to spend time with your partner away from your kids, it can be easier said than done. Maybe you're nursing and the thought of going away overnight makes you feel more stressed than excited. Start with something that's more manageable, like a date at home. Light candles and open a bottle of wine on Friday night, or stay in bed and drink coffee while the kids watch cartoons on Saturday morning. The most important thing is to nurture your relationship in whatever way brings you closer together.

Do you feel that your partner splits the housework 50/50?

44%
Yes

Do you feel that your partner splits childcare 50/50?

53%
Yes

Did your marriage take a backseat when the baby was born?

66%
Yes

Moms need (more) peeps

You have a boss, and a staff, and kids, and maybe a partner and a dog to take care of. Think of friendships as your personal battery boosters that increase your energy, motivation, and wherewithal to do all the rest. From the looks of it, most of us need some serious recharging.

How frequently do you manage to spend time with girlfriends face-to-face without the kids?

10% Weekly

24% Once a month

42% Every few months

24% Never without kids

26%
Have a mom mentor

20%
Belong to a mommy group

40%
Say most of their friends are virtual

Gather your mom tribe

You've got backups for your sitter, backups for you at work, but who's got your back in life? Aside from your partner, if you have one, every working mom needs supportive friends. This is exactly why it's so important to take time to invest in these relationships. Take a look at the following types of gal pals every mom needs and then think about your own circle of friends. You might have a sister who fills more than one category (efficient!) or you might discover a big gaping hole. In that case, you know what to do!

The friend just like you She's got kids the same age, she works, her relationship status is similar. In other words, you're both in the same boat and can relate to each other's ups and downs.

The more experienced friend She may not be older in years, but she's already navigated the trenches you're in now. She's the one who can give you perspective you gain only from hindsight. And she's the one you can really believe when she says, "You will be okay."

The no-kids friend She may be single or coupled up—does not matter. She's your connection to your pre-baby self. She'll keep you up-to-date on the latest celeb gossip, and she'll drag you out for a much-deserved girls' night out.

Completing your circle

Being a mom is hard. Being a working mom can be harder still. And attempting to go any of it alone is not only nearly impossible, it's dangerous too. Without a support network of your partner, friends, family, colleagues, and even acquaintances, you can end up stressed, burned out, and vulnerable. That's no good for you, and it's certainly no good for your kids. So if you feel a familiar well of guilt start to rise the moment you make a date with your partner or your new neighbor down the street, take a breath and remember that you're making an investment in yourself and in your family.

{ mom to mom }

"Having a person to talk with when everything is falling apart helps keep you feeling up. It's the ears listening to your needs for once instead of your kids'."

5

Look Inside

This week's list of triumphs might include getting your kids to preschool for circle time, attending a Pilates class, and achieving professional nirvana when a client approves that never-going-to-end project. You may find moments of joy in unexpected places, as long as you're paying attention.

Take a look inside and ask yourself, "Am I having fun?" This is a big one, and it affects the whole family. Your state of mind—from the moment that little egg and sperm gave a cosmic thumbs-up and decided to form a human being—has had a direct effect on your children. The good news: 82 percent of moms in the *Working Mother* survey said they feel happier since they became parents. Only 4 percent are less happy (14 percent feel about the same). Wherever you fall on this spectrum, upping the happiness factor will make you a better mom. Here are some strategies for tending to your emotional life.

The "good enough" mom

When more moms joined the workforce, we heard all about the "supermom." A revolt against all those high expectations brought about the "slacker mom." Now we're hearing about the "good enough mother," a term coined more than 50 years ago by Dr. D. W. Winnicott, a British pediatrician, sociologist, and psychoanalyst. He said the key role of the good enough mother is to adapt to her baby, which gives him a sense of control and the comfort of being connected with his mother. A mother's attunement to her infant enables him to become more imaginative, playful, and spontaneous—and to grow to be his true self. A mom doesn't need superior skills to nurture her baby, according to Winnicott, just an ordinary ability to tune in to her baby's needs and do what it takes to meet them.

When the term "good enough mom" is used today, it grows out of the idea that most moms have everything their kids need inside themselves already. The good enough mom uses her own best judgment, is available to her child, learns from mistakes, and loves her child, though not necessarily all of his behavior. Unfortunately, today's working moms can have such high—often unrealistic—standards that they can wind up feeling not "good enough" at all.

Keep in mind that there's no single right way to do things, so you don't need to worry that you're doing it wrong and damaging your child. Your baby doesn't need a perfect mom, even if there were such a person. A good enough mom:

● Makes time with her kids a priority. If you're choosing between doing the ironing or playing with your daughter, pick playtime.

● Doesn't compare herself to other moms, especially stay-at-home moms! It may look like their kids are getting straight A's, their homes should be in *House Beautiful*, and they're always cheerful, but you don't know their real stories.

● Accepts limitations. There are no perfect mothers and no perfect children. When we accept our own limitations, we're better able to accept our kids'.

Staying in the moment

One of the biggest working-mother myths about multitasking is that it helps us get more done. This is only the case when the job at hand doesn't require much concentration—like setting the table while talking on the phone. But if your child asks what "s-e-x" means, you don't want to be chopping veggies at the same time. We deplete ourselves when we multitask

"Remember that your children grow up fast. Fifty years from now it won't matter how much money you had or how clean your house was, but your children will remember you for the kind of person you were and for how deeply you loved your family."

Five ways to be present

1 **Spend time with your kids.** No one is better at being present than children. And no one appreciates your total attention as much as they do. Snag minutes together.

2 **Enjoy what you eat.** Eat something that gives you pleasure and savor it. If that something is tiramisu, so much the better! (Dark chocolate has antioxidants, after all.)

3 **Disconnect.** Turn off all electronics for a while, say 2 hours every evening, and reconnect with loved ones and yourself. You'll soon realize how distracting all that background noise is.

4 **Make love.** Sex can reduce stress levels and increase levels of oxytocin, the "bonding hormone." But do you really need science to give you a reason?

5 **Get quiet.** Simply sit, close your eyes, and breathe. Focus on the sensations of breathing and repeat a personal mantra. Slowing down in this way—even for 1 or 2 minutes—helps.

on high-concentration jobs—like when your boss asks you to revise a budget—that's why multitasking can lead to burnout.

The truth about focusing on one thing at a time and living in the moment is that it makes us more productive and happier. Yes, you're pulled in many directions at once, but if you choose to go in one direction at a time, you'll be more effective and less stressed. At work, try to get into what psychologists call "flow," immersing your mind fully in one activity. At home, take time to give your kids your full attention—they need it.

Stress busters

If you're walking around with a stiff neck and a knot in your stomach, and your personality is always set on irritated, it's time to do something about your stress level. This doesn't require 2 hours of meditation daily or locking yourself in an isolation chamber. There are simple things you can do during your day to conquer stress:

Exercise. Yes, we know you're crazy busy. Yes, we know you barely have time to pee, let alone put on your sneakers. Which is why all we're asking is that you commit to 10 minutes. That's it. Do something easy, like walk around the block or flip on a fitness channel and join in. Try to find something you like and stick with it. If you're done after 10 minutes, fine, but chances are, you'll say, "I can do another 10!"

Listen to music. Studies have shown that music can change your mood and reset your emotions. Upbeat tunes beat the blues, and classical tempos soothe frayed nerves. Make a playlist for each of your less-than-desirable moods—angry, fried, panicked, exhausted—and listen to them accordingly. Don't feel obligated to listen to your children's music. A sing-along with Elmo would stress anyone out!

Go shopping with a friend. It's amazing what a little girlfriend time and a shoe sale can do for your sense of well-being. Too

(**survey says**)

How often do you feel stressed out?

59%
Sometimes

35%
Most of the time

6%
Rarely

busy to go out for long? Take advantage of your lunch hour—the freedom it brings is one of the greatest benefits of working.

Laugh more. Watch a funny movie, sitcom, or the latest hit on YouTube. Research shows that laughter produces a positive physical effect as well as a psychological one. Fortunately, this strategy works with kids too.

Get outdoors. Take the family on a picnic in the park, a hike, or a visit to a rose garden. Or simply go for a walk around your neighborhood. Nature is a source of calm, and studies show that you can even benefit from looking at a picture of the outdoors, so display picturesque shots at home and work.

Help someone. Shifting from your problem to another's will help you refocus. Plus, it sets a good example for your kids.

Keeping your cool

From road rage to the insanity of reality TV, we're exposed to a lot of angry emotions. And we all know how short any busy person's fuse can become. Snapping at the kids, coworkers, and strangers in the deli line can become the norm rather than the exception. Blood pressure issues aside, nothing feels worse than losing it. Here's how to keep your apology list as short as possible at home and at the office:

Don't shout back. When you're the target of a toddler tantrum or a crazy colleague, practice emotional leadership. Meaning, prevent yourself from getting angry too. Try the old standbys: breathe deeply and count to ten. To shift your focus, imagine anything that soothes you, like being at the beach.

Get physical. When you're under pressure—plugging away on a particularly difficult project at work, or coping with your child who is going through a "stage"—try to find a physical outlet for your frustration, preferably one that lets you smash and bash things, like kickboxing.

Why it's okay to go to bed when you're actually tired

Working Mother's survey revealed a perfect example of how moms put themselves last. When we asked whether their kids get a good night's sleep on most days, 89 percent said yes. When we asked how much sleep moms are getting, we learned that a measly 6.5 hours a night is the median amount of snooze time. Not everyone needs the same amount of sleep to feel their best, but show us a working mom who isn't tired and we'll give you a hundred bucks. Give yourself permission to go to bed when your body needs to. That One More Thing To Do will still be there tomorrow, and the world will continue to spin!

89%
*My child/children
get a good night's
sleep most nights*

20%
*Kids' bedtimes
7–8 p.m.*

46%
*Kids' bedtimes
8–9 p.m.*

20%
*Kids' bedtimes
9–10 p.m.*

When you feel overwhelmed

Bombarded by demands, expectations, and deadlines, it's easy to feel like we're facing more than we can handle at times. Here's a time-management strategy to keep you from feeling overwhelmed. At work and at home, break down the mass of tasks into manageable pieces, then set priorities. Think of it as taking small sips of a spinach-and-wheat-germ smoothie rather than trying to gulp the entire thing all at once. Here's how to move from paralyzed to powerful:

Make a list. Jotting down everything that you need to get done helps you see the true scope of what you're facing. For each item, write down the steps you need to do to finish, and then focus on whatever the next step is. That's far less intimidating than tackling a broad to-do list. Also look at any tasks that you feel you *should* do but don't want to do. Why not cross them off the list for good? (Feel the weight lift?)

Ask, "What matters most?" Set priorities based on importance and urgency—think of it as mommy triage. Distinguish between what needs to happen today, what can be done next week, and what you can put on a "later" list indefinitely. Too often the urgent-but-not-important tasks get too much of our time and attention.

Focus. Once you've selected a task to complete, practice total engagement. Turn your telephone to mute and take a break from e-mail so you can give it your full attention.

Set time limits. Dedicate a certain amount of time—say 20 minutes—to each task. It can help to set a timer and stay put until you hear the ping unless, of course, you finish faster!

Just say no. Practice saying "no thank you" politely and firmly and with as few words as possible. Whether you're turning down a business lunch invitation or a playdate for your son, don't justify the no with a detailed explanation. Keep it short and sweet. Still not comfortable saying no? Try saying "I wish I could, but"—it's a softer version.

Express yourself. When you feel your emotions building, vent to a friend who's good at talking you down, or simply confide in your dog.

Keep your perspective. Recognize a situation for what it is. If you're fuming because the train is late, again, remind yourself that this is one of the many things that are out of your control. Try to belly breathe.

Limit sugar and caffeine. Too much of these stimulants can leave you feeling tired, cranky, and like a stick of dynamite. Stay hydrated. Taking a sip of water can be amazingly calming.

Worrying less

Fretting over your kids' safety, your career decisions, your relationships, and your overloaded schedule is bound to happen from time to time. But worrying, which can be an appropriate emotion depending on the circumstances, can become destructive when left unchecked. If you feel persistently anxious, call your doctor. In the meantime, try one (or all) of these strategies:

- Write down your worries in two columns: Things You Can Control and Things You Cannot Control. This can help you identify when to try to let go and when to act.

- If journaling isn't for you, try talking it out with your partner or a friend. The goal isn't to dwell on your worries, but to acknowledge them, expose them to the light of day, and let them pass. Think of worries as toxins that must leave your body, then find a way to get them out.

- For the things you can control, or at least influence, such as saving for your child's college education or keeping your family healthy, come up with action plans. Start a college savings account, no matter how small. Make an incremental change in your lifestyle, such as going for a family walk

{ mom to mom }

"You are not alone. There is no such thing as being a supermom who has it all. Stop comparing yourself to every other mom."

"I don't have enough
hours in the day."

65%
Strongly agree

27%
Somewhat agree

after dinner or switching to organic produce. Taking action to battle a fear can help you feel better.

- For the things you cannot control, such as natural disasters, accidents, or the nation's economy, indulge in your fears, but only for 5 minutes. Cry, pace, or stew, and then move on. Visualize your worry by picturing it as a balloon floating away or a log floating downstream. When you can no longer see it, get on with your day.

Self-medication gone too far

A glass of wine takes the edge off worries. A Xanax helps you forget mounting pressures at work. A cigarette from time to time calms your mind. We increasingly hear about successful working moms hiding addictions. But how do you know if you're going too far or if your self-medication habit has turned into a full-blown addiction?

During the past decade, alcohol and prescription drug abuse have been steadily on the rise for women. Alcohol abuse has doubled while prescription drug abuse has quadrupled. Working moms can be particularly vulnerable to these dangerous habits because we tend to have high expectations for ourselves—that we'll remain productive, in control, and composed, no matter what. According to the experts: If you're wondering if your drinking or pill-taking is getting out of control, it probably is. It's time to seek professional help. Call a help line in your community or reach out to an addiction specialist right away.

Staying inspired

Do you introduce yourself as Jenny and Tom's mom or the SVP of marketing? Do you ever introduce yourself as the winner of the salsa dance-off in college? Or the world traveler who has seen the Great Wall of China, hiked in the Andes, and also speaks fluent Italian? How long has it been since you've gone out dancing or planned a trip for yourself? Putting some personal aspirations on the back burner is practical at certain points in life, but keeping them there might eventually cause you to become dissatisfied, even depressed. To stay in touch with yourself:

Connect to your aspirations. Although you might be struggling to find time to brush your teeth and unload the dishwasher, staying linked to your dreams can help inspire you. You may not be able to book a trip to Shanhaiguan right now, but you can keep reading about the Ming Dynasty or watch movies about the Great Wall's history, even if it's only for 7.3 minutes each night before you pass out from exhaustion.

Commit to learning new skills. Mastering French may not be in the cards now, but can you commit to practicing one new phrase a week? Learning something new exercises the brain and slows the aging process. It's a proven mood-lifter and makes you a more valuable commodity, both to your employer and to your family.

Cultivate your passions with your kids. Integrate your love of modern art, surfing, or baking into your children's lives. Visit museums, hit the beach, or decorate cupcakes together (stock up on a rainbow of sprinkles). Talk to them about the things that move you and then include them in your favorite activities. They may not learn to appreciate opera or love baseball, but they'll respect that their mom does, especially if you return the favor and are willing to kick around a soccer ball or play board games with them.

Me time

Do you skip bubble baths because they aren't very relaxing when kids are pounding on the door? Out of guilt, anxiety, or habit, working moms often dismiss the importance of having time for themselves. After all, we may have come to terms with the fact that we enjoy our jobs and that childcare will not harm our kids, but the thought of leaving our children with a

Are you working too much?

It's time to cut back on the hours you log at the office if you nod yes to two or more of the items below:

1 Your boxer barks when you come home—not from joy, but because she thinks you're a stranger.

2 You mistakenly keep calling your sons Frank and Bill, the guy in the mailroom and the new intern.

3 Your family can't understand what you're talking about most of the time. (You think that calling the family together to "ideate" vacation spots is the way everybody speaks.)

4 To you, working a half day means leaving at 6:30 p.m.

5 You refer to the tomatoes in your garden as deliverables.

babysitter so that we can do something as frivolous as go to the latest blockbuster can make us feel irresponsible, even selfish. But the opposite is actually true. Time for ourselves makes us less stressed, more content, and healthier. Here's how to make sure there's time in your life for you:

Make a date with yourself. Block out an hour for an aerobics class on your schedule. Send an electronic invite to a friend for dinner. When you have a date and time on your schedule, you're much less likely to cancel on a friend or yourself.

Go to the doctor. When you set up a wellness visit for your child or make an appointment with the vet, schedule a checkup for you too. Take the whole day off and book a massage, your annual mammogram, and a six-month cleaning at the dentist. Too many moms are great at taking care of their families and then neglect taking care of themselves.

Do like Dad does. You rarely hear fathers talk about being conflicted when it comes to going out with the guys for a beer, booking a ski trip with an old buddy, or spending hours in the garage doing whatever it is that guys do in the garage. This mindset is healthy, and practicing it will help you learn to let go. When your partner makes "me time," you make "me time." If he's playing golf on Saturday morning, you play tennis on Sunday morning. Have each other's back and encourage one another to practice self-care.

Take ten. You might not be able to block off an entire day for pampering like you did when you were single. Nod if you think you're too busy to take time for yourself. You are in good company. Starting today, try to stake out 10 minutes for yourself. Ignore housework and read a book after the kids go to bed, crochet on the bus to work, or call a friend and gossip. Little pit stops like these can help you recharge. Tomorrow, try to take two 10-minute breaks.

Simplify. Zoom in on one thing you really don't like doing—something that takes up too much of your time with too little payoff. If you can afford to, maybe outsource housework every other week, drop off your laundry with a service, or have your groceries delivered. Don't fill the gap with other commitments. Fill it with time for yourself. Suddenly you've got an extra hour to take that jewelry-making class you always wanted to take.

C'mon, get happy

If you've been feeling less than joyful lately and can't quite figure out why, take a few of the following simple actions and see what happens. If you still find that you're persistently sad, irritable, tired, or just don't feel like your usual self, check in with your doctor. Depression is incredibly common among women and can sneak up on you.

{ mom to mom }

"Remember that there's always a shortcut: Shop online, keep great babysitters on speed dial, and don't be afraid to use a housekeeper when you really need one."

Relaxing in real life

Many working moms don't get enough down time, which is why we were happy to see that our survey participants were finding plenty of ways to decompress. Check out their stress-relieving activities below. (Yeah, TV counts. Who doesn't feel better after watching a hilarious show?) Most popular in the "other" category: walk, take a bath, play computer games, pray or read the Bible, and have sex.

51%
Watch TV

48%
Sleep

46%
Work out/yoga

43%
Talk to a friend

43%
Read

24%
Drink wine

13%
Crafts

9%
Meditate

15%
Other

Practice gratitude. At the dinner table or at bedtime, name the things in life that you're grateful for and share them with your family. Encourage your kids and partner to do the same. This trains your mind to dwell on the positive rather than the negative and puts things in perspective. Reframing your thinking to be grateful for what you have, rather than disappointed with what you don't, can have a powerful impact on your day-to-day happiness.

Accentuate the positive. How we express ourselves can affect how happy we feel, and complaining is a fast way to feel down. Look for something positive to say instead.

Make her day. Rather than focus on your own happiness, look for opportunities to make someone else's day. At home and at work, express appreciation frequently.

Smile. Studies prove that thought, emotion, and actions are interconnected. Acting as if you're happy can make it so.

Watch your mouth. Censor what you say in front of your kids. If you talk about how you hate work, they may wonder why you spend so much time there instead of with them.

Happiness Rx

You may feel like you're being selfish when you put yourself first, but it's actually the most generous thing you can do for your child. There is bona fide truth in that old saying, "Happy moms have happy kids." No, they're not going to be blissful every second of the day, and that's not your fault. They're kids, not robots. No matter what you do, you can't possibly prevent all your child's frustrations, nor should you try. Conflict is an important part of life and everyone needs to learn about that. When you show your children that your family values each person's desires and needs (including the need to be alone sometimes), you're teaching them that happiness isn't a personality trait you're born with; it's a skill you can cultivate.

"Just remember that 'This too shall pass.' Keep that mantra close and remember this advice: Spend twice as much time with your kids and half as much money."

6

Mom on the Run

There are going to be days when you can't find your cell phone, one kid starts to cry, the other can't find his blankie, and the cat pees on your report . . . and it's only 7 a.m. You're on the move as soon as you wake up, and the list of things that can contribute to the daily chaos is long for any mom.

But for working moms, there's an extra layer of pressure: You have a lot less time (in some cases, none) to fix what goes wrong. You don't necessarily have the luxury of dropping off a forgotten lunch or stopping to have a heart-to-heart talk when you were all supposed to be in the car 15 minutes ago to make it to soccer practice—and you need to get to the dry cleaners before it closes. Follow these steps and you'll build enough wiggle room into your routine so you'll be able to handle the occasional inevitable meltdown without having one yourself.

Create a command center

The entryway and kitchen are central hubs of activity where a few organizing items can make all the difference.

Assign storage. Create a dedicated spot for each person in the family to stash stuff (coats, shoes, bags, clarinets, whatever). Depending on how much space you have near the door, install locker-like cabinets or simply hang hooks on the wall and place baskets or bins underneath. Label with names.

Charge it. Keep a multi-device charger in the entryway for cell phones, iPods, game handhelds, and anything else that can make you crazy when the battery goes dead.

Use a wall calendar. Keep a large calendar in the kitchen that has everyone's events on it, so that when your second grader tells you that T-ball is switching from Monday to Wednesday afternoon, you can jot it down immediately—in pencil, of course. Go ahead and use electronic or online calendars if you'd like, but keep an old-school paper backup as a visual reminder for the whole family.

Read school news

Talk to your child's daycare provider or school to find out how the staff or teacher prefer to communicate with parents. For example, does your son's kindergarten teacher send home a folder on Friday with all of his projects and notices? Or is there a periodic e-mail that you should pay close attention to? As soon as you know about an event, put it on the master calendar. That way you won't miss Dr. Seuss Day or your client meeting because you had to run back home to fry up some green eggs and ham.

Prep the night before

To give yourself the best shot for a calm morning and on-time departure, start before you go to bed:

- Teach your kids to dress themselves as early as possible. Have them lay out their clothes the night before, and yes, that means that you have to live with their choices unless their selection is inappropriate for school or the weather. The goal is to save time; the bonus is fostering independence.

- If you have a younger child, stock the diaper bag. Once your kids are in school, have them dump and repack their backpacks several times a week. That way, a permission slip doesn't get buried, completed work and school notices come home, and essentials like homework go back. You can double-check behind them, but make it their responsibility. Do the same with your purse and work bag.

{ **mom to mom** }

"If something in your routine isn't working, ask your child for input — really! When kids are involved in making the plan, they're more likely to stick to it!"

- After the kids are in bed, do a quick tidy up of the house, so you can wake up feeling ahead of the game.

- Make lunches and snacks—or better yet, teach your kids how to make their own. Stash acceptable choices, such as string cheese or yogurt, in a dedicated refrigerator drawer. Set ground rules, like requiring them to include a fruit from the bowl, and help them when needed.

- Set up a breakfast buffet—line up fruit, oatmeal, breakfast bars, and cereals on the table along with bowls, spoons, and glasses. A self-serve meal can save precious extra minutes in the rush to get ready.

Become morning people

You hit the snooze at least five times, sleepwalk your way to the shower, and chug a triple espresso to shake off your zombie-like state. You are not a morning person, and neither are your kids. The secret to changing this is earlier bedtimes. Toddlers need 12 to 14 hours of sleep, school-age kids need 10 to 12, and parents need all they can get. Give your kids a lights-out curfew and stick to it. Then give yourself one too. The early-to-bed, early-to-rise routine will help curtail the morning scramble. Rested people are also less cranky and less prone to tantrums and meltdowns. This means you too, Mom!

Find a lost . . . anything

Searching for a missing item can quickly sabotage your schedule. To find something that has strayed, don't ransack the joint. First check where it's "supposed to be" and the surrounding area. Look under things—hat, paper, chair—in that area. Consider the drift factor—did you take it with you when you ran to answer the phone? Sit down and think again. Try the Aha! zone. Most things wander no more than a foot or two from their original location, unless your son decided to use your car keys to start up his Tonka truck. In which case, checking with the kids may shed some light.

Encourage cooperation

Ever notice how behavior issues tend to cycle, often in sync with your biggest deadlines? You'll have a great six months then boom! Suddenly it's The Worst Thing Ever that your child has to go to bed. Whatever the challenge, here's how to deal:

Be clear. Give detailed instructions. Instead of saying, "We're leaving in 10 minutes" (little kids don't really get time frames), ask your kindergartner to put on her coat, hat, and gloves.

Use positive reinforcement. When your child behaves well—say, she gets her backpack organized the night before without being reminded—describe specifically what she did and let her know that you noticed that she's taking care of it herself. The resulting sense of achievement will help cement the behavior and make her feel good.

Be consistent. Kids thrive on routine and knowing what to expect. You don't have to be a drill sergeant, but a few family policies can ease the way. In the morning, it might go something like this: No TV until clothes are on and teeth are brushed. When kids know what's nonnegotiable, there's no incentive to whine, fight, or talk back.

Tricky transitions

Starting something new like changing nannies, switching from daycare to full-time school, or going to camp can be especially sensitive times. Empathy and support will help your child feel more in control. Tips to make any transition smoother:

Talk about feelings. Ask your child what he will miss. With a loss of the familiar and the uncertainty of the future, your child may worry. Let him know that you understand by sharing a similar story of your own and offer extra affection.

Prepare your child. Read some books on the subject, such as stories about the first day of camp. Have him talk to friends

{ mom to mom }

"When you feel yourself *this close* to yelling out of frustration, take a breath and then use descriptive language to tell your kids how you're feeling. For example, 'I'm feeling very frustrated that you haven't put your coats on yet.' Seems weird, but it works every time!"

who have been to camp and loved it. If needed, let him pick out a big-boy lunch box or special backpack for the occasion—he'll take pride in his selection and take ownership of the day.

Keep goodbyes short and sweet. Ease the difficulty of saying goodbye by having a special hug or handshake, but don't drag it out. Long goodbyes are not good for you or your child.

Establish rituals. Make Friday pizza-and-movie night, so you all have something fun to look forward to at the end of the week. Routines provide predictability that can be very comforting to a child who is facing change and to you too.

Work on your game face. Kids pick up even subtle cues from their parents. If you're feeling anxious about a transition, talk to your partner or a friend about your worries.

When the last kid standing . . . is yours

You get a last-minute phone call. A meeting runs late. Your train is delayed. When the unexpected happens, late-pickup fees at your child's after-school program are the least of your problems. What will be a problem is that tear-streaked face when you get there as your child stands alone, the only one left to be picked up. You can already hear him sniffle, "Why didn't you come and get me?" No, you're not the worst mom who ever lived, especially if you approach it this way:

Make some calls. Call to say you're going to be late and ask the caregiver to prepare your child. If you're going to be more than 15 minutes late, call the parent of another child at the facility to see if she can pick up your child. (Make sure you've signed a release form in advance.) If not, speed-dial your backup people.

Model a calm response. Though you may feel like bursting into tears too, what your child needs is for you to be supportive, comforting, and sorry. Explain what happened but don't promise it won't happen again because it might.

Surviving the witching hour

To many working moms, that hour before dinnertime is a perfect storm: Tired, hungry kids collide with a stressed-out mom who feels pressured to do 15 things at once. They want you to look at the hand prints they painted in daycare, the dog won't stop barking, and you still don't know what you all are going to eat. Kick off your shoes, take a deep breath, and follow this step-by-step battle plan:

1   **Give them a snack**
Offer food ASAP. Hungry kids will eat pretty much anything, so think healthy. Keep a bowl stocked with fruit or offer pre-cut carrots, cucumbers, and celery with their favorite dip.

2   **Pay attention**
Your kids need you more than anything else. Make it a ritual to sit down with them while they snack for a little while—even for a few minutes—and let them tell you about their day.

3   **Let them help**
Kids love to feel useful. Even if your toddler can only tear lettuce for the salad or put silverware on the table, she's contributing and being entertained.

4   **Get crafty**
Encourage older kids to get any homework out of the way. This can be a good time for craft projects for younger kids. Keep a basket ready with paper, crayons, and old magazines.

5   **Take shortcuts**
It's perfectly fine to defrost some premade meatballs, announce it's sandwich night, or whip up some eggs and pancakes. Breakfast for dinner? Mom, you rock!

Quality time

Since you won't be spending long weekday afternoons with your kids baking cookies or building a tree house, your time with them in the evening is crucial for all of you. After rushing from work to school to clubs to lessons to getting dinner on the table, your family needs downtime to share, laugh, talk, and play. Sitting at the dinner table texting each other doesn't count. Plopping everyone in front of the TV while Dad checks sports scores on the laptop, Mom answers a text, and the kids fight over the iPad also doesn't count.

Eat together. Try to have dinner as a family at least three times a week. Even once is better than not at all. If you come home too late for dinner, whip up a bedtime snack, or make breakfast your family meal. Studies show that kids who enjoy family meals get better grades, are more likely to stay off drugs and alcohol, and are more physically fit. (Who cares if you bring dinner home in a bag? It's worth it.)

Talk it out. When you have time together with your kids, like during meals or at bedtime, get them talking by being specific. Instead of asking if they had fun at recess, ask whom they played with or bait them with a fun conversation starter: "It's too bad recess was canceled today." Little Sarah will love to tell you why that's not true, in fact, she played tetherball with Henry all during recess and she won two games! Avoid questions that can be answered with a yes-or-no grunt and try to keep it positive, which means no complaining about work.

Set screen-time rules. Enjoying each other's company is next to impossible when the outside world keeps ringing, buzzing, and texting. Set a time each evening to unplug—say from 7 p.m. to 8 p.m. No mobile phones, Internet, TV, music players, video games, or other electronic devices that beep. Use this time to get ready for bed, read, play, swap stories, and reconnect.

Reassure your child. Let him vent about being scared, sad, or disappointed. Explain in simple terms what caused the delay and let him know that you were trying your best to get there. Address his specific worries, however exaggerated: "I would never leave you at school overnight."

Get kids where they need to go

Shuffling kids from baseball practice to Spanish lessons and back for a swim meet can require the skills of an air traffic controller. You've got multiple clubs, sports, and classes, not to mention multiple kids, all looking to land in the right place at the right time. Here's how to avoid crash-and-burn scenarios:

Don't overschedule. At the start of each school term, look at what's doable and think carefully about your family's limits. Is one after-school activity per child plenty to keep everyone happy and you sane? Kids need lots of time to simply play, so you might want to nix chess lessons in favor of playdates. And if you get halfway through the year and realize someone is still overloaded, drop something. No shame in teaching your kids to make healthy changes when they need to.

Carpool. Scout for parents at activities who can help. Offer to coordinate things, giving other parents schedules of who is driving whom on what day. This way, you can schedule yourself for after-work pickups and drop-offs. What you can't do during the week, try to make up for on the weekends.

Ask the leader. See if the coach, teacher, or leader of said sport, lesson, or club would be willing to drive your child home for some extra money.

Find a trustworthy driver. A responsible driver, perhaps a college student whom you know well, may be the answer to your prayers. Pay for the driving time and the gas and enforce safety rules such as only the driver and your kids in the car—all safely buckled up—no exceptions.

{ **mom to mom** }

"When you're chauffeuring your kids, take advantage of the time to talk 'side-by-side.' It's often easier for a child to talk about things like why a friend dumped her when you're not face-to-face. This works especially well with tweens and teens."

The next best thing to being there

Fully 83 percent of working moms we surveyed said they feel guilty when they can't participate in school activities. Fortunately, 74 percent are able to take time during the work day to attend school functions or volunteer at school—but not all the time. Here's advice for tackling thorny school-day challenges:

Daytime events

As much as you and your partner want to be there when your little snowflake twirls in the winter show, sometimes you can't. Send a friend or family member to applaud and film the event. Watch it together as soon as possible, so she can hear you cheer too.

The why-can't-you-ever... questions

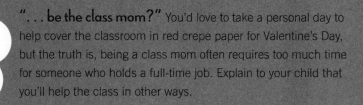

"... be the class mom?" You'd love to take a personal day to help cover the classroom in red crepe paper for Valentine's Day, but the truth is, being a class mom often requires too much time for someone who holds a full-time job. Explain to your child that you'll help the class in other ways.

What you can do Ask the teacher if you could make a guest appearance, perhaps as a surprise reader, or to do a special project like building a birdhouse or planting a container garden. That way your child will feel like you did something special and you'll have to use only half a personal day, so you could come back on another day.

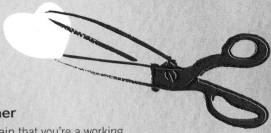

Keeping in touch with the teacher

At the beginning of the school year, explain that you're a working mom who probably won't be able to put in a lot of classroom face time but would like to contribute in other ways. Maybe you can use your scissors skills at night to prep art projects or perhaps you can coordinate volunteers via e-mail in the evenings. It's also important to find out how the teacher prefers to communicate. Some like notes in the homework folder; others opt for e-mails. And don't ever hesitate to raise any concerns you may have.

". . . coach T-ball?" Unless you have a flexible schedule, coaching is too much of a time commitment.

What you can do Offer your child private practice sessions with you. Get out to the park to practice her swing then take her and a few of her teammates out to a professional or college game and enjoy.

". . . be the troop leader?" Most kids wish that their mom would take charge of one of their many extracurricular groups. Unfortunately, most meetings take place during business hours or before you could get there.

What you can do Offer to have the troop over to your house during a weekend. Plan a craft that everyone can do, or organize a volunteer activity or charity event such as a bake sale that donates funds to kids in need.

"As a working mother, my biggest challenge is that the schools operate as if all women are still stay-at-home moms. Maybe I should just send a note at the beginning of the school year that says, 'I'm sorry, but June Cleaver does not live at my house. If you see her, send her over. I have a pile of dirty laundry and dishes that she can do while I'm at work!'"

Getting home late

When you have to log in extra hours at the office, you may feel like you've missed out, not only on the family dinner, but also on precious time with your child. Your child will be missing you too, and will be sure to let you know it. You can ease the pain by creating a special ritual for those times when you get home after dark. Maybe it's making up the next chapter in your special bedtime story together. Or you get to have an after-bedtime snuggle. The important thing is that you turn something that could make you both feel deprived into something special—an excuse to have fun together.

Not guilty

Watch out for times when you overcompensate for mommy guilt. At the end of a business trip, you bring gifts. Another late night at the office means you walk through the door bearing ice cream. "Sure, watch one more TV show, have another cookie, go to bed late tonight"—all because you feel guilt that your child is getting shortchanged of your time. While overcompensating this way may cheer your child up in the short term, it won't teach her how to handle disappointments or difficult situations.

We all want to protect our kids from hurt and pain, but our job is to help them handle all kinds of emotions, including sadness and anger. Rather than offering your child another half hour to watch TV, give her what she really wants—your attention. Have her tell you all about what happened while you were away and do the same for her.

Guilt is a given now and then, but the key is to keep whatever's eating at you in perspective. Did you lose it minutes after walking in the door? Instead of feeling like a failure, remind yourself that you're human. Think about how you'll handle it differently if it happens again, then explain to your child that sometimes mommies make mistakes and need a timeout just like kids. You'll do better next time.

The art of saying no

Working moms are resourceful, creative, and productive individuals. Many are overachievers by nature, so when other parents come by asking for help with the book sale or the fall festival, it's so easy to say yes. You want to be thought of as a mom who participates actively in her child's school, despite having a demanding career. Admit it—you also want that gold star for parenthood. The truth is, working moms have to learn how to say no gracefully. Practice saying it aloud right now: "Wish I could be on the [fill in the blank] committee, but I'm already overbooked." Some other ways to break it to them gently:

Buy time. It may be difficult at first to launch right into saying no, so try delay tactics such as, "I'll have to get back to you" or "Let me check my calendar [or with my partner] and let you know." That way, you have time to think it through and decide if the volunteer work will fit into your schedule.

Use the "not this, but that" maneuver. Offering an alternative keeps you involved without overextending yourself: "I can't bake cookies, but I'm happy to drop off the paper goods."

Be picky. Decide each year which charities you want to support and how many events you can volunteer for. That way when you get an e-mail from the school asking you to organize the annual picnic or a colleague asks you to buy gift wrap for her kid's school, you have some guidelines. It makes it easier to say no if you've said yes to something else or you're planning to help out at another event.

Leave the door open. If you're iffy but want to help, you can hedge your bets by saying that you don't think you can help, but if something changes you'll try. That way, anything you do is a happy bonus.

"I'll have to get back to you."

"Let me check my calendar."

Getting dinner on the table

Dinnertime was often a big source of stress for the moms in the *Working Mother* survey, but they shared some realistic tricks for successful family meals. A few starters: Enlist partners and kids as helpers, cook a fresh meal every other night (fill in with leftovers and takeout), and rely on frozen or premade ingredients for easy side dishes.

"The Crock-Pot is my best friend."

"I cook in bulk on weekends."

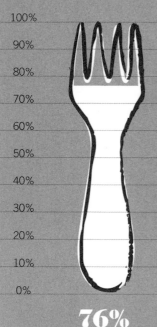

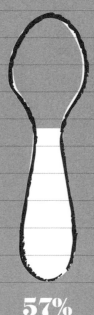

76%
I need shortcuts to make my busy life work.

60%
To get dinner on the table, I keep it simple, or have a set of meals I can cook in 15 minutes.

57%
I feel too rushed to get a healthy dinner on the table most nights.

Leave time to do nothing

Everyone needs downtime. You, your kids, your cat. Time to daydream, play alone, make up silly games with complex rules. Here are some tips on how to make it happen:

Schedule it. Block out "family time"—say Sunday afternoon—on the calendar. Decline all invites during these hours, forget the housework, and focus on savoring these carefree moments.

Unplug. Nix the electronics. Enough said.

Go outside. Explore a new park or your backyard. Don't let the weather keep you inside; invest in rain and snow boots.

Nest. Hang out. Do something together if you want, or go your own way—do sudoku puzzles, read, play with dolls—in peace and quiet. The equivalent of parallel play in toddler terms.

Supply the troops. Teaching your children how to entertain themselves is an essential skill, and giving them the chance to do so is crucial. Have props such as dress-up clothes, building blocks, and pots and pans on hand for pretend play. A blanket can be 100 different things to a preschooler.

A new day dawns

After all is said and done, keeping so many balls in the air is worth zilch if no one's having any fun. Sure, some days are better than others, but there will actually be a time when you will crack up remembering the morning when Jasmine went to kindergarten with a Lean Cuisine and came home with a note from her teacher wondering why your petite 5-year-old is on a diet. Before your head hits the pillow at night, find two or three things you did right. It's easier than you think: Are the kids relatively clean, comfortably warm, and decently fed? Did you show up work and attempt to make a contribution? If so, give yourself a pat on the back and enjoy some much-deserved rest . . . until it all starts again tomorrow.

7

As They Grow

When your kids are little, they worship the ground you walk on, kiss you in public without hesitation, and are always happy to make you a special gift for your birthday, holidays, and sometimes just because it's Monday and you're Mommy! Then come the tween and teen years.

Tweens start testing the I'm-too-cool-for-you waters in public—forget about those goodbye kisses in front of school—but at home, they're all yours. That is, until they're full-fledged teens. At that point all bets are off! There's texting, studying, practicing, and prepping—not to mention raging hormones. Plus a social calendar that's so full you'll have no idea how your son manages to do anything else (but he does). The one thing he probably won't have a lot of time for is you.

Yes, we all know that growing up is about learning how to be independent and happy and responsible. Yes, we want our kids to have all of those qualities, but it's not always easy to get them there. It can be hard to let go when they need us to because, hey, we're moms! We want to help! Here's where a little awareness of what's to come can go a very long way. Consider this chapter your cheat sheet to solving some of the surprising challenges that may lie ahead.

Encouraging independence

Fostering a take-charge attitude in your kids not only helps them in the long run, it also helps you right now. The more they learn to do on their own (or with minimal assistance), the more confident they will become. The fact that the process happens to lighten your load is (almost) secondary. The earlier you start building their skills, the better off you'll all be.

Start young. With your toddler, it can be as simple as having your daughter help put her toys in bins or her empty sippy cup in the sink. It's faster to do it all yourself, but including your child in cleanup—and talking about what you see her doing—begins to instill a sense of responsibility and the expectations you have for family members.

Let kids pick their own clothes. When your son is in preschool, let him get dressed by himself. Give him free rein to choose his outfit, but ask that he lay it out the night before. Resist the urge to criticize his choices. That's probably the fastest way to undermine his sense of achievement. Who cares if his underwear is backward or that his shirt is inside-out? All that matters is that your child is no longer naked.

Allow natural consequences. The game goes up a big notch once your kids hit school, but the same basic rules apply. Your job is to help them discover ways to succeed on their own—not to do it for them. When it comes to homework, for example, you can teach them how to organize their assignments in a notebook, make to-do lists, and break up their work into smaller chunks to tackle throughout the week. But if one night they complain they can't do another minute of homework or they'll die, tell them it's their choice. Will they think the decision was worth it when they face their teachers empty-handed or have to do extra work the rest of the week? Experiencing the bite of natural consequences is a pretty effective way of learning how to make choices. Giving your kids the opportunity to learn from their mistakes is one of the most important things you can do.

Ready . . . already?

One of the more nerve-wracking decisions parents face is when to let their children be unsupervised, whether it's playing

{ mom to mom }

"Talk to your children. They don't need to watch TV or buy things. Sometimes all they want is to talk to you."

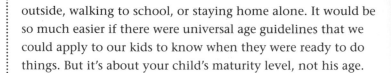

outside, walking to school, or staying home alone. It would be so much easier if there were universal age guidelines that we could apply to our kids to know when they were ready to do things. But it's about your child's maturity level, not his age.

Assess your child solo. Reliable signs that your child is ready to venture out on her own include: Your child pays attention to traffic when crossing the street and doesn't dart out without looking left and right. Plus she's got the other basics down: obeys red and green lights and crosses at corners and not mid-block. That being said, kids aren't ready to walk places alone until around the age of 10.

Add friends to the mix. When your kids start asking to hang out with friends alone, go slow and do test runs. Take your child and her friends to the mall, but have them check in with you every half hour. Kids probably aren't ready to just get dropped off until they are around 12. If your child acts irresponsibly or immaturely, you can pull the plug on these kinds of privileges until she's older and shows greater maturity.

Leave your child home alone. If you're running a 15-minute errand and you have your cell phone and the house doors are locked, it might be okay for your child to stay alone even at 8 or 9—as long as he feels comfortable with the idea. If you're grocery shopping for an hour, maybe age 11 or so. Middle-school age is the earliest a child should go home to an empty house after school, and only if he has shown the maturity to, say, lock the door behind him and do his homework without your supervision. Start with one day a week and build up as he shows his maturity. If you're going out in the evening, 13 is a reasonable age; when your child is old enough to babysit, he's old enough to be home alone in the evening. It's quite possible your incredibly responsible 11-year-old may be ready to be home for an hour by herself while your 14-year-old might leave the stove on and water running while she rocks out on her guitar upstairs. In that case, listen to your gut.

Getting your teen to talk

As children morph during puberty, their personalities get pimples, too. There will be days when the sweet little boy who once refused to let you out of his sight shuns you in public. He'll grunt more than he talks, and the "Do Not Enter" sign on his door will apply to more than his bedroom. Understand that kids often can't explain how they feel. Your main task is to acknowledge their emotions; for instance, say, "You look upset," and then listen calmly. Don't be dismissive or judgmental. Here's how to keep the lines of communication open:

Listen to the small stuff. It's a test to gauge whether or not you can be trusted with the big stuff. If she starts rattling on about why science class sucks, put down the iPad and really listen.

Don't preach. You're going to want to offer your been-there, done-that advice—don't. Teens need to vent. And they don't want a lecture every time they do. If he says, "Tom from biology is such a loser," and you say, "Hey, we don't talk like that," the conversation ends. Try "What did he do?"

Help her find her own answers. Prod her to view things from different perspectives and consider all the consequences of a potential action. Then let her make her own decision.

Pick the right time. Don't flop down on the couch when your son's buddies are over watching the game and ask who's dating whom. Tag your questions onto another activity, washing dishes together or driving him home from a baseball game (that his team won).

Write notes. When tensions are high and you want to end a standoff, write down why you're so angry or frustrated. Leave the letter for your child in her room and ask that she write her response. Expressing one's feelings in writing can feel less confrontational, and sometimes doing it makes you realize that the issue isn't really worth all the angst.

"You just don't understand!"

"My teacher hates me."

"Leave me alone!"

Beware of big-kid burnout

Many teens are involved in so many activities that they make the hottest new celeb look antisocial. There's school, sports, the part-time job, music lessons, tennis camp, the school play, homework, college prep, and the list goes on, leaving little room to relax and lots of room to crack under pressure. In fact, college admissions officers frequently refer to incoming freshmen as "crispies" and "tea cups," meaning that by the time they reach college, students are usually totally fried or delicate to the point of shattering.

Fortunately, your kids have a built-in guide for balancing a hundred things at once. After all, you've been spinning plates at home and juggling burning torches at the office for years! Here's a reminder of how your work skills can help your child:

Teach time management. Even for the Type A's among us, time management is an acquired skill. Pull from your arsenal of tricks and show your kids how it's done. Explain how you create a time line for an upcoming work project, with all of the tasks that need to be completed before the actual deadline.

Also explain that when you're setting priorities, it helps to determine which projects are urgent and which can be taken care of later. The key is to focus on what's important, even if it doesn't have an immediate deadline, and minimize what's not important, even if it feels urgent. When your son is stuck, encourage him to ask, "What's the next step?"

Focus on the process. Your boss doesn't clap and say "Good job!" every time you send an e-mail, so keep it real with praise. Comment on the actions you want to reinforce, but keep it sincere—your kids will know if you're not. Be specific and describe what your child is doing rather than the personality traits they're using to accomplish a task. For instance, note how disciplined your daughter is about studying for her algebra test rather than telling her how smart she is for acing it.

Promote accountability. No one knows better than you that a job is a great way to learn responsibility. Don't protect your child from less-than-ideal work conditions like a strict teacher, difficult boss, or low pay. Listen to how he feels, but don't intervene or try to solve the problem. Your child is the only one who can change his circumstances for the better, even if it's with an attitude adjustment.

Schedule down time. For the mental health of the whole family, schedule a regular movie night, park time, or pajama Sundays when everyone gets to be a slug for a day. If your child has too much on her plate, let her quit. It's okay. Set limits from the get-go on how many extracurricular activities your kids can take on (maybe one club and one sport) and save the rest for next semester.

Sidestep perfectionism. One of the most important lessons you can teach your kids is that not everything has to be done perfectly. Some things you just need to get done so you can move on to the important stuff. And it's absolutely okay to fail. Life goes on. You learn something new. You know what to try differently next time. Model an anti-perfectionist attitude by sharing your own less-than-optimal moments and how those experiences helped you grow.

Speaking of money

As your child becomes more independent, lessons about money—and debt—are essential. Even a younger child can divide up an allowance into categories: save, spend, donate. Have your child practice saving by setting aside money for a bigger-ticket item, like a coveted toy or video game; ease up to saving for college and the concept of *compound interest*. Encourage an older child to earn money, for instance, by babysitting or mowing lawns, and to look for a summer job or internship. Explain how credit-card companies give high-interest cards to students who don't know better and what the term *credit score* means.

{ mom to mom }

"Set a good example when it comes to managing your time wisely. Don't try to tackle every single project or be involved in every activity: Your kids will learn that it's healthy to say no sometimes."

New media traps

Getting into trouble and making less-than-stellar decisions are part of growing up. But given that technology can make mistakes permanent (not to mention public), we parents have a lot of educating—and monitoring—to do. Tell your kids that you are going to check their Facebook pages, blogs, and texts. Simply knowing that will make them think twice before posting online. Only you can determine how closely and frequently you need to monitor your child's online activities, but here are some common scenarios and how to deal with them:

My son won't friend me on Facebook

Ask why—then listen. If he expresses privacy concerns, promise not to post embarrassing things like baby pictures, but let him know that you will occasionally monitor his page. Once he friends you, don't assume that you're privy to everything he posts. Privacy settings allow users to make Friend Lists and restrict access to posts. For instance, your child can tag photos from last night's party so they can be viewed by his "kids from school" list but not by his "family" list. Users can also remove themselves from searches. So your teen can tell you she closed her page, and your searches show that, but her page may still be active for her friends. If you reach this point, ask family friends or relatives to verify that her Facebook page has been closed.

An embarrassing video goes viral

A video of Fido doing a backflip is funny on YouTube. But make sure your kids understand that not everything is for public viewing. Talk with them about the fact that once you upload a video, it stays there. You can take a clip down, but when videos go viral, so many people have copied them that they will be stuck in cyberspace forever. Among the videos your kids should never upload: videos made while they were drunk or engaged in sexual or embarrassing behavior, videos of them ranting about any controversial topic, and—while it seems unbelievable, it's been done—videos of them committing a crime. A good guideline: If they wouldn't want you to watch the video, they shouldn't be in it, much less share it with the cyberworld.

Is my daughter sexting?

Sending explicit photos and messages—also known as sexting—is a common teen activity, but X-rated content rarely stays private in our viral world. So how do you know if your kid is sexting or being harassed by inappropriate photos? You've got to have the talk. Tell your child that sexting isn't allowed and talk about why it's dangerous, including that forwarding a nude photo can get you jail time. That's what happened to middle school students in Alabama who exchanged nude photos of themselves. And it never hurts to learn some texting shorthand, such as MOS (mom over shoulder) and PAW (parents are watching).

My child posted what?!

A kid online has global access to disseminate information—and infinite opportunities to share inappropriate information, especially with the ability to use Twitter, post on sites such as Facebook, and reply to online content. Maybe your child even has a full-blown blog. To protect your child and teach discretion, set firm guidelines. Tell him not to share personal information, including his full name, address, and phone number. Remind him that what he shares can come back to haunt him. College admissions officers and potential employers doing a background check may one day view it.

Distracted driving

Your teen is driving to the mall and she cannot wait to text her best friend about spotting the new guy in class with a mutual friend. On the rise: texting, talking on a cell phone, and engaging in other distracting activities while driving. In a recent poll, a quarter of American teens said they've texted while driving; half said they've been a passenger while a driver has texted. Set an example by never texting or talking on the phone while driving. After all, if it's okay for you to be distracted, even for a few seconds, your kids will think it's okay for them. Have your daughter place her cell phone in a zipped purse or backpack—not by her side in the front seat—so she isn't tempted to text while waiting at a traffic light, and you do the same.

Does your teenager listen to you?

72%
Sometimes

19%
Always

7%
Rarely

2%
Never

Coping with the tough stuff

It's not your imagination: Kids are growing up a whole lot faster than we did thanks to all the media, technology, and unprecedented access they have to peers. Because of that, they face a slew of dangers earlier than ever before. To complicate matters, the biggies—eating disorders, drugs, alcohol, anxiety, depression, bullying, romantic relationships, sex—often come with similar warning signs, making it harder to identify and respond to a problem. Keep an eye out for any abrupt changes in personality, sleep and eating habits, clothing choices, privacy or secrecy, spending, or mood. Some tips for staying aware and available should the need arise:

Have an open-door policy. Explain that if things get sticky, you'll be there to help without judgment. Specify that this includes picking up your child from any location at any time.

Be up-front. Even though openly discussing hot-button topics such as sex can be uncomfortable, it's essential. Don't wait for the issues to arise—set family rules about driving, peer pressure, drugs, and alcohol early so that everyone is clear on what's expected. Help your child think of ways to get out of a difficult situation if he's being pressured to do something unsafe. You don't have to role-play, if that's not your thing, but arming your kids with words they can use to excuse themselves from a negative environment will ease their anxiety (and yours).

Keep close. Studies show that teens are more likely to engage in risky behavior when their friends are watching. So stock the fridge with healthy snacks and encourage your kids to invite their buddies over when you're home so that you can get to know them. There are real perks to having the hang-out house. Keep open communication with their friends' parents too.

Give back. Studies show that children who volunteer even 1 hour per week are less likely than other kids to get involved in destructive behaviors. Volunteering is a great way for a child to feel valued, acquire new skills, and gain a more realistic view of work. Look for opportunities for your child to volunteer, with or without you. Set an example by taking advantage of volunteer or matching-funds programs if your company offers them and talk to your child about what you're doing and why.

Be flexible. Often right before and after a company is sold, there's a lot to be done that requires quick thinking, working on weekends, and all hands on deck. It's temporary, but it's necessary. This can also be true for the tween and teen years. Your child's independence can be misleading—kids still need their parents, especially during rocky times. Be aware that your presence may become more important as your kids get older, which might mean adjusting your work schedule or working fewer hours until a crisis passes.

Remember when

As your kids grow older, every day seems to bring a new challenge. Your 8-year-old asked for her own cell phone (again). Your 10-year-old wants you to ditch the babysitter ("I can handle it, Mom!"). Your 14-year-old? You're not sure what she wants because she hasn't spoken since yesterday morning. Yet despite the fact that childhood seems set on turbo these days, there's a lot that really hasn't changed: school pressure, peer pressure, unrequited love, an unexplainable urge to rebel . . . against anything.

Our job descriptions aren't much different than our moms' either: We have the same challenge of raising strong, confident, independent kids while fighting our own desire to hold on to our babies as long as we possibly can. We worry. We ache when we realize that we're actually not our children's best buddy. But all of that is okay—it's part of the mother growing-up process. Because, after all, what your children really need is someone who sets limits, keeps them safe, and cheers them on. They need a parent—even though they wouldn't be caught dead admitting it.

{ mom to mom }

"It is important to change your expectations as the kids grow up. Every mom has to plan her life according to the stage her kids are going through."

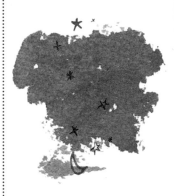

8

Tech Time

You wake up to pee in the middle of the night and check your work e-mail. Yesterday you watched your 18-month-old bark orders into a wooden block as if it were a cell phone. Or maybe you're at the other end of the spectrum: You're perfectly happy leaving tweeting to the birds. Our goal? To get you comfortably somewhere in the middle.

Technology, when used appropriately, can make mothering and working a whole lot easier. In fact, gadgets such as smartphones, laptops, or tablets can help moms get closer to what we all dream about—a way to be in two places at once. Keep tabs through technology. Videochat with your kids when you're on the road. Texting Laney to remind her it's library day works as well as if you were standing right there. A GPS tracker in Tom's mobile shows you his progress walking home from school. The key in all of this is to make sure that you remain in control of the gadget instead of the other way around. Ready to find your happy place 2.0? Here's how to use technology to boost productivity at home and work.

Building your brand

When someone Googles your name, what comes up? If you are nowhere to be found—or worse, a convict with a similar name shows up—your online presence needs some work. The truth is, future bosses and clients will search for your name to see what they can find out. Maintaining a professional online presence is especially crucial for moms who run their own businesses from home. Here's how to get started:

Give yourself a tag line. Identify what makes you distinct from the competition. Find a label that not only describes you, but also that you aspire to. Think beyond your current job title and focus on taking steps to reach the title you'd love to eventually hold. For example, if you're a program manager, you could brand yourself as a "go-to person for strategy."

Set up a website. A website makes it easier for potential clients and employers to see your credentials and contact you. If obvious domain names are taken, such as yourname.com, carefully choose an alternative that reflects your brand. The catch is: Your website must look as professional as you are and be up to date—or it can do more harm than good.

Create an online portfolio. In addition to posting your resume on your site, display your professional work, including any articles you've written and videos of conference presentations. Also consider posting testimonials from satisfied clients.

Blog to promote your brand. To keep clients, future employers, and the general public updated on your field and projects, add a blog to your site, but *only* if you're prepared to maintain it. Few things look worse for a brand than a blog that was last updated six months ago.

Build an audience. Engage an audience by being active on other websites. When you comment on other relevant blogs, include a link to your website.

The social network

The best way to discover career opportunities or professional partnerships is to network—both in person and online. Now that more companies are using social media in recruitment efforts, it's imperative that you're present.

Professional presence Participate in social networks where you have a personal connection, such as professional associations

Momming 2.0

Being a 21st-century working mom means you have access to all kinds of technology that can make your life a whole lot easier to manage. Here's how technology can simplify your day:

1 **App it.** There are apps for almost anything—making your grocery list, following the family spending, entertaining you while waiting in line at the DMV.

2 **Text it.** Need to coordinate who's picking up whom from soccer, violin, and that playdate with the new girl from school? Text your partner to stay on track.

3 **Schedule it.** You still need a master paper calendar of the family's activities, but having a shareable one online can keep you, your partner, and old-enough kids all in the loop.

4 **GPS it.** Or rather, the kids. When your child is ready for a phone, choose one with GPS so you can "see" where she is. Some can even tell you how fast your teen is driving!

5 **Like it.** "Like" your favorite stores on Facebook or sign up for their e-mail lists to get exclusive discounts. Be selective, so you don't waste time sifting through offers that don't interest you.

in your field and through your alma mater. Also join larger professional networking sites such as LinkedIn. Be sure to keep your profile up to date, including a photo and a link to your website. Write a catchy headline—it's one of the first things people will see—and make your profile public. Personalize your URL so that your link is easy to share. Grow your network by linking to colleagues and to those you'd like to meet. Update your status regularly and post links thoughtfully.

Personal boundaries More and more businesses are marketing themselves on large social networks like Facebook. The trick is to maintain boundaries between your professional online presence and your personal one. The easiest way is to maintain two accounts, one that's strictly personal and another strictly professional. Set the privacy settings for your personal account carefully and limit your contacts to a small circle of friends and family you trust. (TMI can kill a job opportunity.) For your business account, eliminate material that isn't directly related to your professional life and never post anything there that you wouldn't want your boss to read!

Hello surfer girl!

Jumping online to shop, chat, or catch up on the news is a great way to escape for a bit. But if you don't pay attention, surfing can suck your time like a Wi-Fi vampire. One easy way to nip an obsession in the bud is to put your online time into your calendar. Ten minutes in the morning, 15 at lunch, 30 when the kiddos are asleep, then shut it down for the day. Already a junkie? You may have to go cold turkey (almost). Give yourself one time a day to surf—that's it. Your allotted time must be after the kids are asleep and when your partner is also otherwise occupied—and it must be 30 minutes or less. You will survive! Trust us.

More of a Facebook fanatic? Facebook is a great way to reconnect and stay in touch with far-flung friends and family, but if you can't remember the last time you had lunch with

{ mom to mom }

"Staying away from technology for just part of the day gave me back so much of my time. I hadn't realized how useful those extra minutes could be."

What's the most recent
technologically savvy skill
you've acquired?

50%
I post to Facebook.

20%
I downloaded an app.

12%
I can tweet.

10%
I blog.

8%
I bought an iPad.

a girlfriend face-to-face, consider carving out time to see your pals in real life. According to researchers at the Mayo Clinic, seeing friends in person can make you happier and healthier.

An added bonus is that seeing friends allows you to pick up on their energy. Most of the information we get in face-to-face communication isn't from the words themselves but from body language, facial expression, and tone of voice. So go ahead and update your status, but use it as a call to action. Let your posse know that you'll be in the park all afternoon with your kids and you want as much company as possible!

E-mail etiquette

When you get an e-mail that makes you want to scream—be it a nasty message from your boss, a dismissive note from your partner, or a sarcastic missive from your teen—do not hit "Reply." Give yourself at least an hour before you respond. Chances are, you should follow up in person to clear the air rather than in a long back-and-forth e-mail exchange. E-mails sent when you're feeling emotional are almost always regrettable, so don't hit "Send" until you're in a better mindset. Friendships have ended, feuds started, and everlasting embarrassment has ensued due to e-mails that never should have landed in the inbox.

To e-mail or not to e-mail

Take into account corporate culture when deciding when and how much e-mail you send at work.

Set boundaries. If your employer considers e-mail a 24/7 activity, it's important to set limits. The goal is to balance after-hours job demands and family time in a way that works for you. You can check to be sure the e-mail isn't an emergency, then answer during business hours or pick certain times to respond, such as once in the morning and once at night. An out-of-office auto-reply is an effective way to let colleagues know when you are unavailable.

Five e-mail to-dos

The hardest truth about e-mail—once you press "Send," there's no turning back. If you send an e-mail to the wrong person, humbly apologize immediately and preferably in person. To avoid similar mishaps, follow this advice:

INBOX

SENT

CHATS

DRAFTS

TRASH

1 Avoid e-mail gossip
You know the saying: If you can't say something nice about someone, then don't say anything at all. Talking—and typing—behind someone's back is a recipe for disaster.

2 Do not "Reply all"
While you may be convinced that all of the parents of your son's kindergarten class should hear your take on circle time, think again. Keep your recipient list as short as possible.

3 Reread
Ever regret dashing off an e-mail? Take the time to proofread all messages and double-check the names of all recipients.

4 Watch your tone
To prevent misunderstandings of your tone, use salutations and a friendly sign-off at the end. It's easy to misinterpret what was meant to be a brief note as unfriendly and curt.

5 Put the recipient in last
Keep the recipient field blank until you've double-checked everything. Alternatively, write your reply in a separate document, then cut and paste it once you're ready.

All a-Twitter

If you don't have a Twitter account—and according to our survey, only 12 percent of you do—it's time to get one. Twitter has become an essential career tool. Start following companies you want to know more about and follow their top executives' or HR professionals' personal Twitter feeds. Creative tweets can help you build a rapport with people who might offer you your next job. Here are some Twitter basics:

1 **Fine-tune your tweet.** You've got 140 characters in which to amuse, inform . . . or bore others. Use humor and stick to colleague-friendly topics, such as an article or a conference.

2 **Use hash tags.** The hash tag symbol (#) is used before relevant keywords in a tweet to categorize them. It helps the tweet show up more easily when people search.

3 **Retweet.** If you come across a tweet that you want to share, the retweet feature ("RT") helps you share the message with your followers. Cite the original author with "@theirname."

4 **Build followers.** Following people on Twitter means you're subscribing to their tweets. To up the chance they, in turn, will follow you, take the time to reply to some of their tweets.

5 **Model top tweets.** To see what's working, look at popular tweets. A good one: "Full of peace and calm this morning. Googled my symptoms and found out I died in my sleep."

Avoid avoidance. When you and a colleague are at odds over something, e-mail can be used to sidestep personal contact. Remember the value of face-to-face or even voice-to-voice communication. If possible, walk over to your colleague's office to talk through whatever you're disagreeing about.

Be respectful. When something devastating has occurred or you have bad news, an e-mail is usually not the appropriate method of communication. Do not fire someone, discuss an illness, or send condolences over e-mail.

Don't expect privacy. Always keep in mind that e-mail you send at work is considered company property and can be retrieved, examined, and used in court. As a rule, never e-mail anything you wouldn't want your boss to read in front of the entire company.

Make it personal. Just as you don't want work e-mails to invade your family time, it's best to answer personal e-mails when you're off the clock. This doesn't always work for moms who run home-based companies or those who use e-mail to communicate with their children during the day. Some companies are more casual than others about this issue. Either way, try to keep personal e-mail to a minimum.

Smartphone addiction

Smartphones—iPhone, BlackBerry, Android, and successors—slide into your pocket or purse like modern Swiss Army knives. Phone, e-mail, calendar, camera—they do it all. These devices are lightweight lifelines for working mothers who can stay connected to the office while out and about and to family when in the office or traveling. Add in music, e-books, games, and apps, and you've got unlimited entertainment at any time. It becomes a problem, however, if you can't shut it off or your toddler tries to hide it so he can have your attention. (Don't beat yourself up too much—31 percent of women in our survey admit to being addicted to their phone.) How to rehab:

{ mom to mom }

"Put away your smartphone when you get home. I promise, work will still be there in the morning."

Set limits. Do you find yourself checking e-mail at red lights, during church, or while playing with your kids? Then it's time to set some boundaries. Turn off your phone for a set period of time, say a half hour, then work your way up to longer chunks such as from dinnertime through your kids' bedtime.

Set the tone. If you're a manager, respect your employees' personal time and e-mail only during business hours. If you can't do that, indicate in the subject header whether the e-mail is "urgent," "respond with 24 hours," or "no response needed."

Set priorities. Does your family tell you they're tired of sharing you with an electronic device? Do you constantly check your computer because you're expecting an urgent work e-mail? Do a gut check about what's most important in your life.

Stronger family ties

Social media sites like Facebook can also help you be a better parent. Show your toddler how much you loved her macaroni necklace and cotton-ball snow family by posting pictures of them. Post encouraging messages to your tween: "That was an amazing touchdown." Be careful not to overdo it or embarrass your offspring.

Social media sites can also help your children keep in touch with you while you're away on business. Use GPS-based apps to check into various locations, and your kids can track mom on the move. Upload pictures so they can see where you're staying and what you've seen. This is also a great time to videochat ("Look, Mom's on TV!") and read that bedtime storybook a little person tucked into your suitcase.

Upload digital shorts, scan in the kids' artwork, and post photos so that grandparents feel like they live next door. Your grade-schooler can post to Aunt Liz's wall each Tuesday to let her know how ballet class is going, but spare your colleagues the details of Timmy's report card by tagging only your family.

Technology for your kids

At what age should kids get their first cell phone or laptop or be allowed to use the iPad? Actually, what age isn't the question to be asking. That's because the answer depends entirely on your child's maturity and emotional development, as well as your own values. Here's a quick rundown of signs that, yes, your kid might be ready to join the tech world:

Cell phones By the time your child is old enough to go places alone, she should be able to handle a phone. However, you still need to keep tabs and limits on whom she can call and whether or how often she can text.

Laptops There's nothing wrong with even a preschooler having a computer as long as you limit the amount of time he has on it and the type of content he can access. This rule holds true until he escapes to college!

iPod or equivalent Any child who has time-management issues may need limits when it comes to playing music. Creating playlists can be time-consuming; however, if you've got a Responsible Ruby on your hands, let her groove away. No matter when you give the green light, stay away from earbuds, which raise the risk of hearing loss.

Technology is a mom's best friend

The whole point of having these electronic devices is to make our lives easier—not more complicated and certainly not more stressful. How wonderful is it that now you can look at your baby from a thousand miles away and read her a story, track your child's walk home from school and know he's where he's supposed to be, or text your tweens about when they'll be home and get a nearly instant answer? All you have to do is keep tabs on you. If losing your Droid falls on your list of "Worst things that could ever happen," it's time to rethink. After all, working moms were kicking butt just fine for decades without all the fancy-pants help!

{ mom to mom }

"Use technology to your advantage. Playing word games on the iPad with your little ones could help you relate to them once they begin tweeting."

9

Navigating
Now

For working moms, weeks, months, even *years* can fly by without us really noticing whether we're where we want to be. With *so* much to do, we can find ourselves on autopilot trying to get as much done as we can while staying semi-sane at work and at home. There's nothing wrong with navigating that way, as long as every once in a while we turn the mombot off and do a flesh-and-blood status check on life right now, today.

Take a week or month (when you're not blind with exhaustion or stressed to the hilt with a big project) to look at where you are at this very moment in your career. Think broadly about whether it's making sense for you. Are you happy? Are the kids? Your partner, if you have one? The answer may be obvious, and if it's a clear "Yes!" that's great. If it's not, it's time to do some reflecting and information gathering.

Talk to your family, including kids who are old enough to weigh in. Get a fresh perspective from a girlfriend or a career counselor. The goal, as always, is to find the right mix of work and everything else that will give you the happiness you deserve. With 71 percent of working moms in the *Working Mother* survey reporting that they feel torn between work and family, help can't come fast enough. This chapter will give you the tools, strategies, and advice you need to get wherever it is you'd like to be, if not today, then at the very least, soon.

Taking time off

For some of us, work loses its luster when there's a new baby and we want to stay home, even if we were sure we would want to go back to work. Or maybe your baby is now in junior high and needs you around more. Missing out can feel even worse when things at the office are less than inspiring or extra taxing. If you're stuck in a rough patch, you might want to consider taking some time off or making a change. Before quitting in tears the next time Junior says a new word to Miss Mary at daycare before he says it to you, take an honest look at the situation. Aside from the current and long-term financial analysis of whether you can stop working, afford current living expenses, and save for the future, ask yourself:

Is that grass really greener? Try your hand at being a stay-at-home mom during time off when your family is not on vacation or traveling. See what it's like during the average ho-hum week alone with your little one. Besides exhausted, how do you feel? Ready to sign up? Or eager to get back to the office with an increased respect for moms who stay at home?

What can I change? Look at your schedule, workload, vacation time, and salary. Ask yourself what is stopping you from loving the job you have. Can you transfer within the company? Hire help? Ask for a sabbatical?

What will you lose? Look at the job market in your field and talk to other moms who have opted out of the workforce. Ask them how hard it was to try to get back into their career after taking a break. Consider what time away will do to your earning potential once you return to work.

The new face of flex

So you've asked yourself all the questions, and you ran the numbers. If it turns out that staying home isn't going to be the best option for you, explore the possibility of a nontraditional schedule with your boss. The most common arrangements are:

{ mom to mom }

"Don't doubt yourself if you're a single parent, and don't lower your standards. I got divorced and went back to school — while working full-time — when my son was two. Because I did, I was able to get better jobs and ultimately work at home and enjoy my son's teen years."

Did you ask for a flexible
or part-time schedule after
your maternity leave?

64%
No

36%
Yes

Flextime Employers who embrace flexible schedules understand that one-size-fits-all work hours don't always make the most sense for employees, especially working parents. Employees who have flextime frequently have leeway in configuring their own work schedules, such as being in the office from 7 a.m. to 3 p.m. instead of the typical 9 to 5. There's often a certain time period during which managers want all employees on hand for meetings, usually between 11 a.m. and 3 p.m., but other than that, employees can often customize their hours.

Compressed workweek This benefit allows employees to work more hours on some days in order to take off time during the workweek. For example, you might work longer hours for 9 days and have every other Friday off. Having a full day off during the workweek while preserving a full-time salary offers loads of advantages, especially if you have a long daily commute. You can take care of errands, go to appointments, volunteer at school, and have more time for fun on the weekends with your family.

Telecommuting Aka working from home, telecommuting provides workers with the ability to electronically link to the office from almost anywhere. The basic idea is that work is something you do, not necessarily something you travel to. How frequently you telecommute depends on your job, but 2 days per week is the average in the United States according to the International Telework Association. Once you've proven yourself to be dependable and hardworking (of course, you are!), this is a great perk to ask for.

Job share Job-sharing allows two people to split one job and one salary. You could each work half days, alternate days, or split the week. Finding the right partner is crucial—you must have a strong working relationship and ethic—but when it works, it works. And because you've got built-in coverage, you're almost never called in on your day off.

Make yourself indispensable

When you've got a good gig, you want to make sure you'll keep it, no matter what's happening with the economy. The key is to make your manager believe she can't survive without you. Here's how:

1 **Think bottom line**
Be the go-to gal for money-saving—or generating—ideas, whether it's making double-sided copies or bringing in a big client. The resourcefulness of motherhood gives you a leg up!

2 **Manage up**
Make your boss look good by identifying and compensating for her weaknesses. Is she disorganized and often late? Be über-organized, be on time, and (gently) remind her of deadlines.

3 **Take on tasks**
There are always important jobs that nobody wants, such as summarizing meetings. When you can, raise your hand and your visibility by tackling these tasks with a smile on your face.

4 **Be info central**
Keep password-protected contact lists that are valuable to your company. Update them often and be the go-to person when anyone is looking for what's-her-name's number.

5 **Get out**
If you want to be viewed as more than a desk-bound drone, spend face time with people in your company and industry. Supplement e-mails with phone calls and personal visits.

Work from home — and get things done

Whether you work from home occasionally or run a business from your basement, there's a lot to love about breaking free of the office. You get to wear sweats all day. There's no commute. You don't have to listen to that gum-cracker. Working from home does come with its own set of challenges. Check out some of the biggest and how to handle them:

1 Distractions, distractions, distractions

Because many a home office is a desk and a laptop in a room that pulls double duty, it's easy to get distracted by the "house" stuff to do. The lure to do a little organizing can soon turn into a half-day project—and not the one that you're being paid for.

What to do Use bookcases, curtains, and screens to physically define your work area. That way, when you're in this space, it will be easier to stay focused.

2 Isolation

Lots of people thrive on the dynamics of an office, and you won't know how much you do until you're out of it. Telecommuting comes with another downside: You may be left out of unplanned brainstorming or crisis-management meetings, which can lower your profile at work.

What to do Develop solid relationships with others who work from home. Schedule lunch with your locals and keep the lines of communication open with your colleagues. Check in often to stay up on the daily buzz.

3 Interruptions

Just like at the office, you'll still have to deal with people popping by. Unfortunately, "Mommy's working" won't prevent your kids from asking if you know where their socks are or your partner from texting you to please pick up the dry cleaning.

What to do Train your family to understand that being physically home doesn't mean that you're available. Set guidelines such as don't interrupt unless it's urgent, don't touch any office equipment, don't answer Mommy's cell phone, and keep noise levels down during work hours.

4 Procrastination

With no boss looking over your shoulder, you can work at your own pace, strike when genius hits, and let your creative juices percolate. But it can also be far too easy to procrastinate.

What to do Create a personal work schedule and develop your self-discipline muscles. You may need more structure than when you're at the office. Take your calendar and assign specific tasks to specific blocks. Reward yourself when you stay on top of it.

5 Gadget addiction

You may find yourself constantly checking your gadgets to stay in the loop. The problem is, that urge can spill into family time, leaving you less connected with the ones who matter most.

What to do Take e-mail breaks. Let colleagues know that you won't be checking your inbox while you work on a project and that they can call you if something comes up.

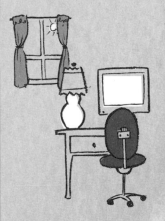

What's great (and what's not) about being a working mom

There's a lot to love about this life, but everything has at least a few downsides. As long as the pros outweigh the cons, you're on the right track! Take a look at how many of the moms in our survey agreed with the following statements:

What's great

84%
Working with creative people

80%
Setting a great example for my kids

62%
Having a meaningful career

58%
Being financially independent

57%
Having an independent life apart from my child

56%
Fulfilling myself professionally

What's not so much

92%
Not having enough hours in the day

79%
Being stressed with having so much to do

71%
Feeling torn between work and family needs

66%
Being unavailable to my child sometimes

Stretch

When you're trying to figure out your next best move, taking on a stretch assignment that expands your skills can help. Volunteer for a high-profile project or for a short-term assignment in a different part of your business. If you're leaning toward staying, a project that stretches your abilities can reinvigorate you, not to mention keep you front and center for a promotion or more interesting assignments. One caveat: If you're already stretched to the max, this isn't the time to seek out more work. Do what you can to get your current load under control and save the expansion for later. However, a promotion is an exception. Don't automatically assume you're too busy to take on more responsibility. Look at it as an opportunity to negotiate for better hours, a job description that works for you, additional staff, and, of course, a higher salary. Factor in that more money can open up different childcare options, like a top daycare center or a nanny.

When to look for a new job

After several years, your boss is still calling you Jenny instead of Gina. She doesn't understand why you would stay home because your child has pink eye. Employees hired after you are getting promotions. You're bored. You're angry. You're starting to use more and more sick days. Guess what? It sounds like it's time to look for a new job. Before you go rogue, consider these ways to get the process going:

Reach out. Discreetly connect with everyone you know, from other parents watching the swim meet to fellow alumni. Talk about what kind of work you're looking for and your openness to new opportunities. Ask for names of others who could help. Be sure to follow up.

Revise your resume. Update and pump up your resume by making sure it's not just a list of tasks. Does your resume show how you are a valuable employee? Does it highlight all the benefits a company will gain from bringing you on board?

{ mom to mom }

"On my first day back at work after maternity leave, I quit. They wanted me to go on a week-long business trip the next day."

Explore. Strategically think about the right next step. Do you want to find similar work or branch out? What is best for your family? Think about short- and long-term options.

Connecting with confidence

Some people are born networkers. They can chat up their boss's boss as easily as a new parent at a PTA meeting. Others need to work at it. It's well worth the effort, especially if you're looking to make a change. Mastering the art of small talk is an essential business skill. It can help you expand your circle of connections and give you a wealth of new people on your side, ears to the ground. If walking up to someone and introducing yourself gives you a knot in your stomach and a frog in your throat, try these tips:

- Think ahead. If you feel prepared with something witty to say after you exchange hellos, you'll be less anxious.

- Keep up with current events and bestsellers. See the blockbuster movies and watch an episode or two of the top TV shows. Check out what's popular on YouTube and Twitter. Stay versed in hip restaurants, theater, and museum exhibits. This is all fodder for your post-hello transition.

- Practice. Chat up the cashier at the grocery store, the senior in the post office line with you, the teenager at the doctor's office. When you're used to making small talk with people who don't seem intimidating, it's easier to schmooze with those who do.

- Take notes. When you hear a funny story or joke, your child says something that made you crack up, or you've told an anecdote that was a hit, capture it on paper.

Rescuing a bad job interview

Congrats! You've landed an interview for a dream job. You've prepared. You've researched the company and been briefed by

Making the most of a job you love

We focus on change in this chapter, but we know plenty of working moms who truly enjoy their jobs and want nothing more than to grow within the company. The good news is that one out of every four working moms we surveyed have professional mentors who provide advice and guidance. Some companies are taking this concept one step further with sponsors, senior execs with the clout to groom and advance their protégés. Here's how to find a mentor or a sponsor:

Consider chemistry. Think about your personality and the types of teachers you've enjoyed working with. Are you drawn to powerful high-energy types or are you inspired by quiet intellects?

Be strategic. Look for someone you think you will learn from versus someone with the most impressive title. Take the advice that you would give your child when looking for someone to play with at the park.

Get the word out. Ask people in your network. Be open-minded about gender, distance, and even industry. Some of the best advice can come from a person with a different perspective.

Be creative. Think of the smartest person you know, then invite her to lunch and get her talking about her mentors. Ask if she knows anyone who might be a good match for you.

Don't limit yourself. Seek out and surround yourself with successful people who are willing to offer insight and advice. Think of this group as your own board of directors.

a friend who works there. You're impeccably dressed—down to your lucky underwear—but the guy who's interviewing you has glanced at his watch so often you want to rip it off his wrist. He seems to be reading your resume for the first time, and he isn't impressed. Here's how to salvage the interview:

Remember your goal. You really don't need to land the job right now. You need to make it to the next round of interviews.

Wake up your audience. Drop an attention-getter into the conversation, such as some surprising industry news. Then get back to business and talk about a project at which you excelled.

Act like a politician. You have kids, you know the drill: If you're asked a question that you don't want to answer, change the topic. "That's a good question. It reminds me of how I landed my firm's biggest client." And you're off and running.

Be confident. It isn't what you say, but how you say it. If you are asked a difficult question, say, "I don't know, but I'm a quick study," rather than stumbling through an incoherent response.

Resigning without burning bridges

Cue the trumpets! You've received an offer you can't refuse. Now it's time to share the news with your boss. There's an art to quitting, and the "take this job and shove it" attitude has no part in it. Here's a strategy to leaving without having any doors slammed—or locked—behind you:

Be careful explaining why you're leaving. Saying "An amazing opportunity has come my way that I can't ignore" is acceptable. Saying "I've found a manager who isn't a toxic, micromanaging narcissist" is not.

Be flexible about your last day. Give at least two weeks notice: It's customary and professional. If a new employer is pressuring you to leave earlier, don't do it. Leaving a boss in the lurch is a bad move. If you're leaving to start your own business or to freelance, you'll likely have flexibility here and your employer could be your first customer! Try to squeeze in time off between gigs if you can to recharge and spend time with the kids.

Keep in touch. Your coworkers and managers are people who know how good you are at what you do. Invite them to lunch. Have coffee when you can. The goal shouldn't be to gossip about the old gang (okay, maybe a little), but to build a solid network of friends in high places.

Making peace with change

Taking a time-out to think about how things are going on a deeper level can be a little scary, especially if you find that it's time to make a change. But you know what? It's an adventure too, and that not-knowing-what's-going-to-happen-next feeling can be pretty exciting if you let it. When you feel your heart start to race, take a breath and remember that what's ahead is a huge opportunity to be creative and grow.

For all the uncertainty a brand-new path creates, in the end, it almost always leads someplace better. Hopefully, it will be quite obvious when you arrive, like when you've got an amazing new boss who cares about what you say and works hard to keep her team motivated. Or when you (and your manager) realize that your job-sharing or telecommuting trial is totally working and the practice run becomes permanent. Other times, you have to hack through some vines and branches to realize you're there.

What counts is that you got yourself out of a less-than-great situation or made a good one better. The goal is to find a career direction that leaves you inspired, challenged, and most of all, happy. Sure, you may have to navigate some side roads and back ways to get there. Who cares? You will learn more with each twist and turn, getting you closer every day.

{ mom to mom }

"Don't stay at your job because it's 'safe' if you aren't really happy there. If your job makes you miserable, take the plunge and find another one."

10

Work Anywhere

Moms are redefining what it means to be a "working mom." Gone is the woman in the navy-blue suit holed up in her office from 9 to 5. In her place we see everyone from the stiletto-wearing financial analyst who works crazy hours on Wall Street to the home-based jewelry designer sporting a hoodie who sells her wares on Etsy. Today, you're a working mom if you say you are. End of story.

Technology, talent, and some employers' progressive thinking are not only making it possible for women to choose what they want to do—from anthropologist to zoologist—they're also giving many working mothers control over where and when they work. Cut free from an office, a cookie-cutter corporate climb, and a "How can you work and be a mom?" prejudice, many moms are reaching new heights in the workplace—and facing new conundrums.

Some mothers have employers or jobs that don't allow them to work remotely or have flextime. For other moms, having more control over their careers isn't as idyllic as it sounds. Some women who telecommute report that working remotely is harder because their boss and colleagues scrutinize their results much more deeply than they did before. And no matter what your situation, there will be difficult choices to make and conflicts to resolve. But unlike the generations who shaped the workforce before us, we are getting more opportunities to draw our own road maps and decide where we want to go.

Pacing your career

Just as childhood has different phases of development, your professional life does, too. When your children are young and actually want to be with Mommy, you may choose to "dial down" your career, opting for a less time-consuming position, the flexibility of consulting, or the opportunity to stay at home, if that's an option for you. When your kids become more independent, you may have the energy and drive to return to the workforce, "ramp up" your career, or go for that big promotion with more responsibility.

This doesn't mean that working moms no longer have to juggle, but there are more ways to make that juggling a little less draining. Maybe flextime allows you to drop off your daughter at preschool at 9 a.m. and arrive at work at 9:30—a half hour that makes all the difference in how you start your day. You can telecommute on Fridays and spend your lunch hour volunteering at your son's school. Stuck in bumper-to-bumper traffic during an important conference call? Call in from your car—with a hands-free device, of course.

More and more, working moms are able to self-regulate the intensity and direction of their careers, choosing when to slow down or zoom ahead, freelance or work in an office, accept a promotion or take time off. Having this kind of control over when, where, and how much you work can help make you healthier, too. In fact, research suggests that people who have some flexibility in the workplace enjoy greater physical and mental well-being than those in more rigid jobs, as well as lower blood pressure, better sleep, and less daytime fatigue.

Setting boundaries

You're not doomed if you happen to work for a company with less flexibility. Instead, your goal could be to do your best to keep your boundaries between work and home firm. We know, this is easier said than done, so here's the first step— simply give yourself permission to draw the line. No one else

{ mom to mom }

"Sometimes, despite your best efforts, you find your work and family lives aren't humming along as you'd hoped. If you can't get the changes you need, it may be time to leave your position. Sometimes the answer is a new job. Sometimes the answer is a new boss. And sometimes the answer is becoming your own boss."

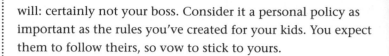

{ **mom to mom** }

"Don't assume you can't change your hours. Ask about telecommuting options! It has helped me with balance and feeling connected to my kids."

will: certainly not your boss. Consider it a personal policy as important as the rules you've created for your kids. You expect them to follow theirs, so vow to stick to yours.

On the horizon

When flextime started creeping into the workplace, it seemed revolutionary and getting to work for a company offering it seemed about as likely as hitting the lottery. You may feel the same way when you learn about the new options that are starting to pop up, but something tells us it won't be too long before they become as expected as flex.

Results-only work environment Under this arrangement, employees can work wherever and whenever they wish, as long as assignments are completed on time. Mandatory meetings don't exist. Face-time pressures don't exist. The only goal is to get the job done however you best can. Best Buy's corporate headquarters originally launched this approach, but other companies such as Gap and IBM have since adopted it.

Workshifting This is all about our ability to work almost anywhere thanks to the Internet. If you're more productive from a park bench, that's where you should crank out your sales presentation. If you need to polish a report while you wait for the sitter to arrive, that's fine too. Employees and their employers have discovered that changing surroundings can put you in a better mood and increase creativity and productivity. What working mom couldn't use more of all three?

Mass-career customization This program allows employees to make fundamental changes in their workload, responsibilities, job location, and scheduling without fearing they'll lose their job. Deloitte, the international accounting and consulting firm, created this program to reflect its belief that employees are more satisfied (and thus more loyal and likely to stay) when they can fit their life into their work and their work into their life. The company is taking employees' needs seriously and

Out-of-office work etiquette

Working wherever and whenever comes with some tricky situations—awkward conference calls, weak Wi-Fi, and "Oh, no, the battery is dying" scenarios. These are things most of us didn't have to contend with while working within the confines of four walls with a land line. Here are some dos and don'ts to help make things a bit smoother:

Do plan ahead for conference calls. Be sure to send relevant material to your colleagues 24 hours in advance. During the call, avoid general questions like, "Any comments?" It can be difficult to know who should jump in and respond. Instead, ask specific people for feedback. Try to end your calls with a brief summary and next steps.

Don't ignore the lens when videoconferencing. When speaking to a camera, make direct eye contact with the lens (it's tempting to look down at the screen so you can see your colleagues' faces) and enunciate. Microphones pick up rustling paper and barking dogs—so it's polite to mute your microphone when others are talking. As time delays are common, only one person should speak at a time.

Do know how you'll handle dropped calls. Dead zones can lead to a hair-pulling game of phone tag. Instead, establish this rule of thumb: The person who initiated the call is the one who calls back.

Don't overstay your welcome at Wi-Fi hotspots. It's great to get a change of scenery from your home office, but when you use a local Wi-Fi hotspot, there are some rules. First, don't take up more space than you need. Second, order food and/or drinks. Third, get to know the manager and thank her when you leave.

Do let calls go to voicemail. Just because your phone rings doesn't mean it's always appropriate to answer it. Hit "ignore" in the elevator, the bus, or the train, and anywhere else space is limited between you and the strangers around you. Instead, send the caller a text indicating when you will be able to return the call.

Be your own boss

If you're thinking about striking out on your own, you're in good company. The number of women-owned businesses is growing twice as fast as the number of male-owned businesses. In *Working Mother's* survey, one in ten working moms were self-employed. This isn't just a trend, ladies; it's a movement! Think you'd like to be your own boss? Here are the signs that you're ready:

1 You're comfortable with some risk, including giving up the consistency of weekly paychecks. Launching any new biz takes some time, so having funds set aside to see you through the start-up phase is critical.

2 You've done your research *and* found your twist. It seems obvious, but you've got to have pretty strong evidence that there's a market for your product or service, and that you're going to have something new and cool to bring to the market.

3 You're committed for the long haul. The road to becoming a successful entrepreneur can be bumpy. After all, about half of all small businesses fail within 5 years, according to the Small Business Association. Realize that stumbling blocks and failures may dot the road on your way to success. Having a long-term plan—and a lot of support—will help you stay the course.

4. You're self-motivated and confident. Nobody will be watching over your shoulder if you procrastinate. You will have only yourself to please. You need to be driven and have the self-discipline to be your own boss. You will likely not only work long and hard but will also need to sell yourself and talk up your business. If you don't feel comfortable self-promoting, this may not be for you.

5. You're a healthy worrier. Too much anxiety can be paralyzing. But if you thoughtfully replay things in your mind and look for ways you might do something better next time around, you'll drive your business forward. People who tend to rest on their laurels often overlook opportunities or fail to see potential pitfalls.

6. You're flexible. You are someone who likes change and adapts quickly. You don't mind if things don't always go according to plan. In fact, to you, shaking things up is fun, not frustrating.

7. You see the world how it actually is, rather than how you think it should be. Optimists are welcome but you also must be a realist. A key strength will be your ability to step back and assess with clear eyes what's working and what's not.

creating a culture where flexibility is the norm. The trend could be hitting your company in the future.

Form a support group

If your company doesn't have one already, ask about forming an employee resource group (ERG) for moms. These support groups are growing in popularity as ways for employees who share certain similarities—such as ethnicity, skill set, or life circumstance—to support each other and look for solutions to common barriers they face. As part of a group, you can share ideas and help effect company-wide changes. The payoffs for you are company visibility and the chance to establish policies that help working moms do their best work.

Something else to consider: Mix a little business with pleasure and start an informal working moms' group. Maybe it's as simple as shooting an e-mail to all your working mom pals inviting them for drinks once a month. For fresh perspectives, encourage your pals to bring their working mom friends too. Spending time with people who totally get what your life is like is a huge stress reliever, and it can also be seriously fun.

No apologies

Ever get a raised eyebrow when you say you have kids and you work? (Unfortunately, you can't win either way—stay-at-home moms get the same look for not working.) If you're asked about your choice, it's good to have a response ready that will stop them cold. A line like, "Why raise my child when someone else can?!" or "My baby is just for show" will shut down a critic in a heartbeat. Too snarky? Try this honest (and still dramatic) answer the next time someone asks how you can work outside the home when you have a young child: "I work so that my child *has* a home." Pause while this sinks in, then continue, "I also work because I find it fulfilling and because I want to be a positive role model." Judging is a competitive sport among some women. It just is. What. Ever. If, where, and when you choose to work is nobody's business but your own.

Embrace change

The modern work landscape can feel overwhelming at times, with so many shifts occurring on a daily basis. More women are working than ever before. For some, the fields in which you work are also changing. For others, pressure comes from the desire to gain new skill sets and take on stretch assignments so that you can climb to new heights. What if you'd like to coast for a little while? We're creatures of habit, after all.

The key here is to recognize if you're hanging on to the status quo because you're afraid of the unknown and don't want to fail. If so, give yourself a pep talk. Think in terms of small steps forward. Leaving your comfort zone may turn out to be a great experience. Go on Twitter and open an account. Start blogging. Talk to others who are flexible and observe how they live their lives. Are they clinging to one way of doing things or zigging and zagging along with the changes? And when you feel you're losing courage, think about what Charles Darwin, the famous naturalist, said: "It's not the strongest of the species that survives. It's the one that's the most adaptable to change."

Working moms rising

It's energizing to see the traditional work model explode, giving moms more enticing and flexible job opportunities than ever before. In the United States, women—millions of individuals with a voice and the power to advocate—now outnumber men in the workplace. Not that we're out to steamroll the guys, but it's important to recognize that we finally have reached critical mass and can not only demand change, but see to it that it happens. Of course, having a career sometimes feels like an Outward Bound survival course, but it's also an adventure that can take you places you never imagined. That is, as long as you ask for and accept help along the way. Supportive employers, trusted mentors, and other working moms who have been there have the wisdom, insight, and shortcuts that can allow you to run around a whole lot less and enjoy the life you're building a whole lot more.

Index

a

allies *(see support network)*

anger management techniques
66, 69

b

babysitter 52, 55

back-to-work preparation 24

being late 82, 85, 88

boss, management of 17, 44–45,
48–49

branding yourself 106–107

breast pump 32, 34–35

c

career strategies 125–129, 133,
134, 138

change 129, 139

chaos control 78–80

child cooperation 81

child independence 79, 94–96,
99

childcare
decision flow chart for 20–21
support network for 41, 46,
52–53, 82
survey results about 33

command center 78–79

compressed workweek 120

d

depression, postpartum 31

dinnertime strategies 83–84, 90

down time 99

dress for success 16, 19

e

e-mail etiquette 110–111, 113

employee resource group 138

exercise 65

f

Facebook 100, 109, 114

family time 91

fatigue, strategies at work for
41–42

favor-bank deposits 53

financial decisions 19, 23

financial literacy 99

flextime 120, 133, 134

focus 63–65, 68

g

gadget addiction 113–114, 123

girlfriends 58–59, 65–66

"good enough" mom 46,
62–63

gratitude 75

guilt 32, 36–37, 88

h

happiness 62, 73, 75, 118

healthy food tips 15, 42, 47

i

independence 79, 94–96, 99

insurance decisions 19

isolation 25, 122

j

job interview tips 126, 128

job-sharing 120

l

legal decisions 19

lost items, how to find 80

love life 56–57

m

making yourself indispensable
121

mass-career customization 134,
138

maternity leave
  back-to-work preparation
    during 24
  considerations during 25–27
  employer's policies on 14
  negotiation of 17
  work wind down before 18
me time 71–73
media traps 100–101
meetings
  last-minute 40–41
  sneaking out of 43
  staying awake during 41–42
mental health 31, 62–63, 99
mentors 127
mistakes, strategy for handling
  47
multitasking 63–65

n

nausea 14, 16
negotiations 17, 44–45, 48–49
networking
  social 107, 109–110, 114
  work 125–126
new job, connections for
  125–126

o

online posting, inappropriate
  100–101
out-of-office work etiquette 1
  35
overwhelmed, strategies to
  reduce feeling 68

p

parenting decisions 19–21
postpartum depression 31

pregnancy
  exercise during 16
  fears about 23
  hydration during 16
  recommended foods during 15
  side-effects of 15
  sleep requirements during 15
  telling your boss 14–15
preparation 79–80
procrastination 123
promotion 125

q

quality time 84

r

relaxation 74–75
resignation tips 128–129
results-only work environment
  134
returning to work
  childcare considerations
    32–33, 41
  decisions about 26–27
  emotional considerations
    30–32, 36–37
risky behavior, teen 102

s

saying "no" 68, 89
school activity participation
  86–87
self-employment 136–137
self-medication 70
separation anxiety 31
sleep requirements
  for children 67, 80
  for pregnant mom 15
  for working mom 67, 80

smartphone addiction 113–114
social networking 107, 109–110, 114
sponsors 127
stress reduction 65–66
stretch assignments 125
support network
    for childcare 41, 46, 52–53, 82
    at work 138

t

taking time off 119
talking with your child 79, 81, 82, 85, 97
talking with your teen 97, 102–103
technology
    addictions 113–114, 123
    branding 106–107
    e-mail etiquette 110–111, 113
    Facebook 109, 114
    keeping track with 108
    for kids 115
    social networking 107, 109–110, 114
    Twitter 112
teen burnout 98–99
teens, risky behavior 102
telecommuting 120, 133
texting, inappropriate 100–101
time management
    for teens 98
    for moms 79–80, 99, 108
transitions
    changing jobs 128–129
    strategies for children 81–82, 85

transportation for child's activities 85
Twitter 112

u

understanding
    promoting at home 72, 81, 97, 101, 123
    promoting at work 44, 109, 120, 125

v

volunteering
    at school 87–89, 102–103, 120, 130
    at work 52, 126

w

woman-owned businesses 136
work
    advancement 125
    alternative schedules 119–120, 134, 138
    boundaries 133–134
    finding a mentor or sponsor 127
    last day strategy 128–129
    negotiations 17, 44–45, 48–49
    out-of-office etiquette 135
    results-only environment 134
work-from-home strategies 122–123
working pros and cons 118–119, 124
working too much 72
workshifting 134
worrying, strategies to reduce 68–70

Acknowledgments

A grateful thank you to the incredibly talented and thoughtful team at Weldon Owen—Terry Newell, Roger Shaw, Elizabeth Dougherty, and Katie Moore—who made our idea a reality; to Elizabeth Shaw and Abbie Tuller for fine-tuning the text; and to the design team—Kelly Booth, Michel Gadwa, Conor Buckley, and Marisa Kwek—for making the book look so beautiful.

Thank you to *Working Mother*'s Barbara Turvett for sharing brilliant ideas and insights, and to Ebby Antigua, Ryan Cline, and Ilisa Cohen for going above and way beyond. Thanks to India Cooper for her eagle eyes and Lee Clower, a photographer we love. Our deep gratitude to Nishan Akgulian for capturing in his illustrations everything we wanted to say. A special thank you to Carol Evans, president of Working Mother Media, for her support and belief in this guide's value to working moms.

A shout out to Walker Communications' Paule Anne Kaziewicz for helping us craft the survey. And to the thousand-plus working moms who participated and shared priceless pointers.

To our backup teams—family, friends, and caregivers:

A huge thank you from Suzanne to Wendy and Nancy, for their unwavering support. Thanks to my wonderful parents. And to my husband for his belief in me and his encouragement.

And from Teresa, a thank you to Mary O'Rourke, Kathy Reiper, and Sharon Curley who never fail to come to my rescue. To my sister Mar for her mad micromanaging that saves me daily. And to Mike for making parenting fun.

And to our sons, Jack and Jay, you keep the "survival" fun with your irresistible charm that reminds us that no matter how busy we are, there's always time for a tickle fight.

Working Mother Media

2 Park Avenue, New York, NY 10016

www.workingmother.com

President *Carol Evans*

Weldon Owen Inc.

415 Jackson Street, San Francisco, CA 94111

www.wopublishing.com

President, CEO *Terry Newell*

VP, Publisher *Roger Shaw*

Executive Editor *Elizabeth Dougherty*

Project Editors *Elizabeth Anne Shaw* and *Abigail Tuller*

Assistant Editor *Katharine Moore*

Creative Director *Kelly Booth*

Designer *Michel Gadwa*

Illustration Coordinator *Conor Buckley*

Cover Designer *Marisa Kwek*

Production Director *Chris Hemesath*

Production Manager *Michelle Duggan*

Color Manager *Teri Bell*

Illustrations © 2011 Nishan Akgulian: Cover, back cover, endpapers, and pages 1–4, 7, 12–14, 23, 25, 27–31, 37–42, 45, 47, 50–53, 55, 59–63, 65, 69–73, 75–80, 85, 88, 91–98, 103–107, 110, 113–119, 125, 129–134, 139–142, 144.

Decorative patterns courtesy of Shutterstock and Michel Gadwa. All other illustrations by Conor Buckley.

Working Mother Media and Weldon Owen are divisions of Bonnier Corp.

Library of Congress Control Number: 2011928850

ISBN 978-1-61628-147-2

10 9 8 7 6 5 4 3 2 1

2011 2012 2013 2014

Printed by Toppan-Leefung Printing Ltd. in China.

Claim your subscription to *Working Mother* now!

Thank you for your purchase of *Working Mother's Working Mom Survival Guide*. Included is a 1-year subscription (8 issues valued at $9.00) to *Working Mother*, the magazine for career-committed mothers.

Fill out and mail this paid subscription voucher to begin receiving your subscription to *Working Mother*.

Terms & Conditions:

If you're already a *Working Mother* subscriber, a 1-year extension to your subscription will be included with your $14.95 purchase of *Working Mom Survival Guide*. There are no hidden charges or automatic renewals. You will never receive a bill for this subscription. Please allow six to eight weeks for delivery of your first issue.

Offer valid for U.S. subscribers only. Limit one subscription per household, family, or address. Offer expires 12/31/12. Please note that your name and address that you provide will be handled in accordance with *Working Mother's* privacy policy, which can be found at http://www.workingmother.com/privacy-policy. If you prefer not to receive this magazine and would like a rebate for the value instead, please *print* the word "rebate" on this form, fill in the information on the back of this card, and mail it along with a copy of your purchase receipt within 30 days of purchasing the book. Your rebate will not be processed without valid proof of purchase. Checks will be sent within 12 weeks of receipt of request.

Other Restrictions:

Limit one promotional subscription per customer per household/family per address. We reserve the right to end the promotion at any time.

How this Promotion Works:

Included with your purchase of *Working Mom Survival Guide* for $14.95 is a 1-year (8 issues, $9.00 value) subscription to *Working Mother* magazine. Fill in your name and address and mail to:

> Attn: Working Mother Partnerships
> Palm Coast Data
> PO Box 422260
> Palm Coast, FL 32142-2260

Yes! Start my subscription to *Working Mother.*

Name _____

Address _____

_____

City / State / Zip _____

X10MSG

E-mail Address _____

May we have permission to communicate with you via e-mail regarding your subscription? __Yes __No

Working Mother

As the voice of over 2.2 million working moms, *Working Mother* acts as a community for women who work and raise a family. The magazine offers a unique blend of personal, professional, and family-related editorial content and advocates for the issues that matter most to working moms. The *Working Mother* 100 Best Companies initiative has become a benchmark for corporate America, and the groundbreaking Best Companies for Multicultural Women initiative has drawn national attention to issues of gender, race, and diversity in the workplace.

Suzanne Riss

The former editor-in-chief of *Working Mother* magazine, Suzanne (left) is an award-winning journalist with 15 years of experience developing content for women. An expert brand builder across print, broadcast, and digital media platforms, she writes regularly about parenting, health, lifestyle, and financial issues. Suzanne has held senior positions at many national magazines and holds a master's degree in journalism from Columbia University. In her 5 years as the editor-in-chief at *Working Mother*, she fielded hundreds of questions each week from working moms seeking guidance as they navigated their complex lives.

Teresa Palagano

A writer and editor for the past 15 years, including 8 years at *Working Mother*, most recently as executive editor, Teresa (right) writes regularly about parenting, health, and lifestyle issues. An award-winning journalist, she has held senior positions at many national magazines, covering everything from the wine industry and magazine publishing to spa treatments and shoes. Teresa is most happy when helping working moms confront the mind-boggling realities of parenting today.

Michele Borba, EdD

The mother of three sons, Dr. Michele Borba is a parenting expert and educational psychologist who is a regular contributor to the *Today* show. An award-winning author of 23 books, she most recently wrote *The Big Book of Parenting Solutions: 101 Anwers to Your Everyday Challenges and Wildest Worries*.